Commentary on the Ḥizb al-Baḥr

Commentary on the Ḥizb al-Baḥr of Imam Shādhilī

by
Shaykh Aḥmad Zarrūq

Translated by Khalid Williams

VISIONS OF REALITY

Published by

First Edition

The book is printed on acid free paper of archival quality.

Printed and bound in the United Kingdom

Thanks are due to:
Khalid Williams (Translation)
Abdassamad Clarke (Design and Typesetting)
Muhammad Ridwaan (Editing)

ISBN 978-1-909460-02-7
Book Distribution All Enquiries:
sales@visions-of-reality.com
www.visions-of-reality.com

VISIONS OF REALITY

بسم الله الرحمن الرحيم

Contents

Publisher's Note ix

Brief Biography of Sidi Ahmad Zarruq ﷺ xi
In the Early Days xi
His Youth xv
His Travels xvii
Shams al-Din al-Jawjari xvii
Imam al-Sakhawi xviii
Shaykh Ahmad ibn Uqbah al-Hadrami xix
Sidi Ahmad Zarruq
Monitor of Scholars and Saints xx
The Journey to Misrata xxii
Karamat of Sidi Ahmad Zarruq xxiv
Sidi Ahmad Zarruq's Heritage xxv
A final story to illustrate visitation
to the *maqam* of Sidi Ahmad xxvi
Works of Sidi Ahmad Zarruq xxvii
Details of Some of the Works of Sidi Ahmad Zarruq xxx

About *Hizb al-Bahr* *xxxiv*
The Story of the Origin of the Blessed Prayer
Known as the *Hizb al-Bahr* Litany of the Sea xxxv
Recitation of the *Hizb al-Bahr* xxxvii
Commentaries on *Hizb al-Bahr* xl
Sidi Ahmad Zarruq's *Sharh Hizb al-Bahr* xli

Introduction 1

INTRODUCTION – PART ONE 4
The reality of litanies and their purpose, rules, and related matters 4

INTRODUCTION – PART TWO 17
The requirements for composing a litany and using it, and the proper intention of the one who composes it and the one who uses it, and the ruling of this and matters adjacent to it 17

INTRODUCTION – PART THREE 27
Why this litany is called the 'Litany of the Sea', why it was composed, how it should be used, the rulings of travel by sea and the special qualities of the sea 27

The *Ḥizb al-Baḥr* of Imam Shādhilī ﵁ 32

Commentary 43

CONCLUSION – PART ONE 87
Concerning the issue of belief, criticism and imitation 87

CONCLUSION – PART TWO 89
The valid areas of imitation, what it brings, and its ruling 89

CONCLUSION, PART THREE 92
How conduct should be imitated 92

SOME CONCLUDING ADVICE 94

ADDENDUM 102
Some important matters that people following the spiritual path require, whether they be in the world of isolation or the world of means 102

A FINAL WORD 120

Publisher's Note

It is with great pleasure that we present the translation of Sidi Ahmad Zarruq's 'Commentary on the *Hizb al-Bahr*.' Sidi Ahmad Zarruq was one of the most outstandingly brilliant scholars to emerge from the Maghrib. An expert hadith scholar, considered the authority in the Maliki school, and an authorised Sufi Shaykh.

He travelled widely and studied with the most authoritative scholars of his day excelling in both the outward sciences of the Shariah and the inward sciences of Tasawwuf. He was an original writer who demonstrated his mastery in numerous commentaries that he wrote. This current work is the translation of one such commentary *Sharh Hizb al-Bahr*.

As the teachings of Abul Hasan al-Shadhili take root in the newly emerging Muslim communities in the West, the need for literature in English is paramount.

As such it is our hope that this work will be of benefit to its readers and encourage others to produce more works of Sidi Ahmad Zarruq – may Allah be well pleased with him.

I am indebted to Sidi Iyad Ghouj of Dar Al-Fath Research and Publications for kindly bringing to my attention and allowing me to have a copy of the *Sharh Hizb al-Bahr* (which has been drawn from the original manuscripts) and also to Sidi Tahir Kasmani and his wife Suemyya Gangat for their involvement in this project. I also owe Professor Ghulam Shamas ur Rehman sincere thanks for allowing me use of his yet unpublished thesis *A Critical Edition of Qawa'id al-Tasawwuf* which I have relied on especially for biographical information and details of Sidi Ahmad's works.

Amjid Illahi

Brief Biography of Sidi Ahmad Zarruq[1] ﵁

"On the whole his worth is beyond description. He who devotes himself to record his experience, counsels and letters will make a whole volume out of them!" Ahmad Baba al-Timbukti

In the Early Days

"I was born at sunrise on Thursday 22nd Muharram 846AH[2]. My mother passed away on the following Saturday when she was twenty three years old and my father the following Wednesday in his thirty second year; his father[3] had died six days before my birth in his fifty third year. Then I lived under the protection of Allah with my grandmother Umm al-Banin."[4]

So writes Shaykh Shihab al-Din Abu al-Abbas Ahmad ibn Ahmad ibn Muhammad ibn Isa al-Barnusi al-Fasi (d. 899AH/1493CE) known as Zarruq (his grandfather had blue eyes

1 Based on Khushaim's *Zarruq the Sufi* and Prof. Ghulam Shamas ur Rehman's *A Critical Edition of Qawaid al-Tasawwuf* PhD, Exeter University 2009
2 June 7th 1442 CE
3 i.e. Sidi Ahmad's grandfather
4 Shaykh Zarruq, *al-Kunnash* p11

– '*azraq*' typical of the Berbers – which led to the family name Zarruq) in his autobiography *al-Kunnash Fi' Ilm al-Ash*[5].

He belonged to the Berber tribe of Baranis who were inhabitants between the cities of Taza and Fez the latter of which was to give him the *nisbah* al-Fasi.

Although he was named Muhammad he became known by his father's name as Ahmad – a name that he loved so much that he was to name his four sons so[6].

His parents died in an epidemic days after his birth leaving the new born an orphan to be cared for by relatives. Although left in the care of his paternal grandmother – he was actually brought up by his maternal grandmother, Umm al-Banin.

Sidi Ahmad Zarruq considered his grandmother Umm al-Banin to be an expert scholar as well as a saint[7] who was well connected with the leading scholars in Fez at that time. Umm al-Banin was also a student of the celebrated scholar Abu Muhammad Abdullah al-Abdusi[8] and friends with his two sisters Umm Hani

5 *An Anthology in the Science of Anything*

6 He cites three reasons for keeping the name Ahmad firstly because he became familiar with it, secondly this name had not been twisted and mispronounced by the common folk and thirdly because this is the name that none of the other Prophets had and it was by this name that Jesus, peace be upon him had foretold the good news about the coming of Sayyiduna Muhammad peace and blessings be upon him in the Quran

7 Umm al Banin – this saintly lady is referred to as 'a saint, a righteous and pure woman' *Tabaqat al-Shadhiliyah al-Kubra al-Hasan ibn Muhammad al-Kuhin*

8 Al-Sakhawi: 'He had a very sharp memory and was a mufti of the Maghrib al-Aqsa Imam of Jami al-Qarawiyyin. He was a master of jurists and Sufis. He was a teacher of many renowned scholars like Ibn al-Amlal the researcher, al-Quri the jurist, and Abu Muhammad al-Wiryaghli and many others' see al-Timbukti, *Nayl al-Ibtihaj* p84 whilst al-Suyuti in his *Ayan al-Ayan* records 'He was prominent scholar, expert and pious man and he was a mufti of Fez'.

and Fatima – both of whom were known for their command of jurisprudence. Sidi Ahmad, who would visit al-Abdusi frequently with his grandmother, was to state later that Shaykh al-Abdusi was responsible for removing heresy from the Maghrib whilst implementing the rules and regulations of the Shariah.

Umm al-Banin lovingly raised Sidi Ahmad, teaching him herself and was to be of great influence on him, as he recalls in his autobiography[9].

"She told me that one night, when I was two years old, I looked at a star and asked who put it in the sky. She explained to me the duty of belief in that matter. She would tell me anecdotes about the righteous and the reliant ones. When she told me stories she never told me anything except about the Prophet's miracles and the wonderful miracles of the devout." So the love of Allah, His Rasul ﷺ and the Awliya'Allah (the Friends of Allah) was instilled in him at a tender age.

"Encouraging me to pray she would put a dirham on my pillow, so that I might see it when I opened my eyes in the morning. She would say 'perform the Fajr prayer and then take it'. Her idea was that the dirham would help me to pray and keep me away from corruption and prevent me from looking at what is in other people's hands when I desire to buy something".

"She instructed me how to pray, and ordered me to do so from the age of five. At the same age she sent me to the Kuttab[10] (Quranic school) and started teaching me about *tawhid*, trust, faith and religion by a very curious method. One day she prepared food for me. When I came back from the *kuttab* to lunch she said 'I have got nothing for you. But provision is in the Almighty's treasury. Sit

9 Shaykh Zarruq, *al-Kunnash p11*

10 There were some two hundred of these in Fez at the time

down and let us ask Him.' Both of us stretched our hands towards the sky and began praying. Then she said 'Go and look, maybe Allah has put something in the corner of the house'. We began to search and how glad I was when I found the food! She said 'Come and let us thank Allah before we eat, so that our Lord may give us more from His grace'. We thanked Allah and praised Him for an hour, then commenced eating. She would do the same many times till I grew up."

Being raised by such a saintly woman was to have a profound impact on Sidi Ahmad who even as a child had signs of maturity beyond his age. On an occasion he sat in the market place to listen to the storyteller when his grandmother's uncle came to him and said "Nobody sits here except the idle" – he never did that again for the rest of his life[11].

At the Kuttab he was regular, quiet and studious. He memorised portions of the Quran daily completing the entire Quran at the tender age of ten.

Sidi Ahmad recollects his grandmother saying "Surely you must learn the Quran for your religion and a profession for your livelihood" – to that end she apprenticed him with a local cobbler. The sense of not relying on others and earning for one's own upkeep was an important feature in Sidi Ahmad's life, protecting him from the blight that others suffered by becoming 'official government scholars'.

Thus as al-Kuhin noted "she…brought him up on a path of proper direction and perfection, so that he grew up enjoying acts

11 Similarly Umm Hani al-Abdusiyyah once saw his hands and feet dyed with henna she commented on it being a woman's mark – he never dyed himself after that.

of devotion and worship…[12]"

Umm al-Banin died when Sidi Ahmad was ten years old but her saintly influence would stay with him for life.

His Youth

At the age of sixteen he joined the famous Jami'at al-Qarawiyin and the Madrasah Inaniya where he studied the traditional Islamic sciences including Maliki jurisprudence, theology, hadith and Arabic grammar. It is clear from Sidi Ahmad's autobiography that at this stage of his life he was studying with the most eminent scholars at one of the most respected educational faculties in the Muslim world. This was to be a feature in his life – the young Ahmad Zarruq would travel widely and be blessed with opportunities to sit with leading luminaries of the age as he recollects:

> "Allah transferred me to a life of study and learning at the age of sixteen. So I studied *al-Risalah* of al-Sahnun,[13] under the guidance of Ali al-Satti and Abd'Allah al-Fakhkhar, and Quranic studies, research method and argumentation from a group of eminent scholars. Among them, there were al-Quri[14] and al-Zarhuni, who were very pious men, al-Majasi, and Ustadh al-Saghayr Abd'Allah al-Tujibi (d.887/1482) who

12 al-Kuhin, *Tabaqat al-Shadhiliyah p.123*

13 Sahnun ibn Sa'id ibn Habib al-Tanukhi (d. 256AH) a student of the students of Imam Dar al-Hijra, Imam Malik. Sahnun's most famous work the *al-Mudawanna* is one of the greatest works in capturing the knowledge prevalent in Madina al-Munawara in the early generations.

14 Abu Abd'Allah Muhammad b. Qasim b. Muhammad al-Lakhmi al-Meknasi al-Quri (d. 872/1467) was from al-Quri, a city near Ashbayliyah, Andalus and settled in Morocco. Al-Quri was a distinguished Maliki faqih and teacher at the celebrated al-Qarawiyyin and a mufti of Fez. Shaykh Zarruq studied with him and was even a guest in his house. Shaykh Zarruq had many discussions with al-Quri who, alongside teaching fiqh, would also teach the works of Ibn Ata'Allah al-Iskandari.

was an expert of the Nafi' version of recitation[15]. Then I indulged myself in the studies of Sufism, scholasticism and theology. I learned *al-Risalah al-Qudsiyah* of al-Ghazali and *al-Aqa'id* of al-Tusi from al-Shaykh Abd Rahman al-Majduli who was one of the students of al-Ubayy[16]. Then I studied some part of *al-Tanwir* of Ibn Ata'Allah al-Iskandari and most of the parts of *al-Sahih* of al-Bukhari and *al-Ahkam al-Sughra* of Abd al-Haqq and *al-Jami'* of al-Tirmidhi from al-Quri whilst I accompanied lots of distinguished, blessed learned men, and many jurists and ascetics." [17]

He also started to write at this stage – at the age of twenty four (in 870AH) penning his first two works: a commentary on the *Hikam* of Ibn Ata'Allah al-Islandari and a collection of sayings of the Awliya' Allah called *Tuhfat al-Murid.*

The other person to have played a significant part in the life of the young Ahmad Zarruq was Abu Abdullah Muhammad al-Zaytuni – a blind African Shadhili Shaykh with enormous force of character. He was head of the Zawiyah Bu al-Qutut[18] in Fez. Al-Zaytuni was attested with numerous miracles and he was known as the 'blind serpent'[19] for the efficacy of his prayers. Many stories exist of al-Zaytuni's warding off burglars, bandits and thieves.

15 One of the canonical Quranic recitations.

16 Famous Maliki jurist and hadith scholar from Tunis whose works included a much respected commentary to the *Sahih* of Imam Muslim, *Ikmalu Ikmali'l-Mu'allim,* as well as a commentary on the *Mudawwanah* of al-Sahnun

17 Al-Timbukti *Nayl al-Ibtihaj* p85

18 It was originally built by Abu al-Hasan ibn Ghalib (Sidi Ali Boughaleb) – an Andalusian hadith scholar and Sufi adept of Ibn al-Arif (d.536/1121). Sidi Ali Boughaleb was also a teacher of Sidi Abu Madyan al-Ghawth having taught him the *Jami'* of Imam Tirmidhi in Fez.

19 Ibn Askar al-Hasani, *Dawhat al-Nashir*

Sidi Ahmad was to spend time in the Zawiyah Bu al-Qutut and also travelled with Sh Zaytuni to visit the *maqam* of Abu Yaza Yalannur b. Maymun (d. 572/1176) – the Shaykh of Abu Madyan al-Ghawth[20] in 870AH.

His Travels

By the age of twenty seven both Shaykh al-Zaytuni (d. 871AH) and Shaykh al-Quri (d. 872AH) had died, Sidi Ahmad then set out on the journey to Hajj. En route he stopped in Cairo meeting and studying with notable scholars and Sufis[21].

After Hajj he spent a year in Madina al Munawwara, and as ever, every opportunity to study was utilised. Sidi Ahmad mentions his studies in the Hijaz with the eminent Maliki faqih Nur al-Din Sanhuri[22] (d. 889). The journey homewards continued with a year in Cairo where he was to meet amongst others Shams al-Din al-Jawjari, Imam al-Sakhawi and Shaykh Ahmad ibn Uqbah al-Hadrami.

Shams al-Din al-Jawjari

Zarruq writes in his autobiography: "al-Shaykh Shams al-Din

20 Sidi Abu Madyan Shuayb ibn al-Husayn al-Ansari a renowned Sufi master and Maliki faqih was born in the suburban town of Cantillana near Seville, in Muslim Spain around the year 509/1115-16. He was orphaned at a tender age and worked for his brothers as a shepherd until an overwhelming desire for religion drove him to study the Islamic sciences in Morocco. He continued to travel Eastwards towards Baghdad where he met his Shaykh Ghawth al-Azam Shaykh Abdal Qadir Jilani.

21 "I met al-Shaykh Nur al-Din al-Tanasi in Cairo and participated in his lectures and studied some books under his supervision. He had a great command of knowledge and language and possessed great qualities. He died in 875AH whilst I was in the Hijaz" *al-Kunnash* p38

22 "He was the leader of the Maliki school of law in his time" Makhluf, *Shajarat al-Nur* p.258

al-Jawjari (d. 896-1490/91) was a Shafi'i jurist, grammarian and theologian. He had a commentary on *al-Shadhur* of Ibn Hisham and a commentary on *al-Tanbih*. I studied some books of al-Mahalli[23] under his supervision"

IMAM AL-SAKHAWI

Muhammad ibn Abd al-Rahman al-Sakhawi (831-902/1427-1497) was an eminent scholar of the Shafi'i school, a brilliant hadith scholar and a student of the outstanding Shaykh al-Islam Imam Ibn Hajar al-Asqalani, as well as being in the Shadhili Tariqa. Shaykh Zarruq studied with al-Sakhawi who issued him with an *ijazah*. We know what Shaykh Zarruq meant to Imam Sakhawi by the entry that he gave him in his monumental biographical dictionary of prominent ulama *al-Daw' al-Lami'*.

"He (Sidi Ahmad) travelled to Egypt and then he went to the Hijaz to perform the pilgrimage. He resided at Medina for a period of time. Then he settled in Cairo for about one year and learned Arabic and theology constantly from al-Jawjari and others. He

23 An Egyptian scholar of the Shafi'i school who wrote treatises on law (*fiqh*) and legal theory (*usul al-fiqh*), including a famous commentary on al-Juwayni's short manual of legal theory, *Kitab al-Waraqat*. He was a recognised scholar whose most famous work was a partial Quran commentary covering sura 1 and suras 18-114, which his student Jalal al-Din al-Suyuti completed to form the famous "Commentary of the Two Jalals". Interestingly Imam Suyuti was a contemporary of Sidi Ahmad and both were Shadhilis. Suyuti's book *Tayid al-Haqiqah al-Aliyah wa-Tashyid al-Tariqah al-Shadhiliyah* (a translation of which is in preparation for publication) demonstrates his strong affiliation with the Shadhili Tariqa. In many ways Sidi Ahmad Zarruq and Imam Suyuti represent the Shadhili Tariqa at the time both were Ashari in aqidah – with the former representing the Maliki school and the latter (who was a *mujtahid* Imam in the Shafi'i school) representing the same from the East (Egypt) – needless to say both their fames were global and their works are still in circulation centuries later.

read *Bulugh al-Maram*[24] and comprehended its terminologies under my supervision. He accompanied me in certain things and I benefited from a group of his fellow countrymen." Interestingly al-Sakhawi also noted "...he was mostly influenced by Sufism."

Shaykh Ahmad ibn Uqbah al-Hadrami

Taj al-Din Abu al-Abbas Ahmad ibn Uqbah al-Hadrami (824-895/1421/1489) – a sufi Shaykh from Hadramawt, Yemen who had established himself in Cairo and was the leader of the Shadhili community there.

This was the man who was to transform and have an everlasting impact on the life of Sidi Ahmad Zarruq for this was Sidi Ahmad Zarruq's shaykh in the Shadhili Tariqa – this was the man that Sidi Ahmad "...took hands with him, received the litanies, was inspired through him, received spiritual guidance from him, attached himself to him, and stayed with him. He was his Shaykh and only confidant on the Path..."[25]

Sidi Ahmad was to spend eight months in the company of Shaykh al-Hadrami and the two forged a close connection. Shaykh al-Hadrami was to give his disciple some lines of poetry when asked for advice:

"Submit to Salma and go wherever she goes,
Follow the wind of destiny and turn wherever it turns"[26]

Sidi Ahmad mentions that Shaykh al-Hadrami would recite these lines whenever he would visit him and adds that 'I understand that Salma is the Shariah'

24 A famous Shafi'i work by Ibn Hajar al-Asqalani about the use of hadith in Shariah rulings

25 al-Hasan ibn Muhammad al-Kuhin, *Tabaqat al-Shadhiliyah al-Kubra* p.124

26 Ibn Askar al-Hasani, *Dawhat al-Nashir*

Shaykh al-Hadrami was keen for Sidi Ahmad to return to the Maghrib and so at the age of 31 in 877 AH he set out to return to Morocco, staying in close contact with his Shaykh by correspondence. He was accompanied by a friend Sidi Muhammad al-Khasasi. The journey was to take some two years travelling along the Mediterranean coast with numerous sojourns in various places where meetings with scholars took place. In Tripoli he was to meet the Qadi of the city – regarded as one of the foremost Maliki faqihs, Abd al-Rahman al-Yazliti al-Qarawi[27] (d. 875AH) known as Halulu. He also studied with Abul Abbas Ahmad b. Yunis al-Tunsi (d. 878AH) another Maliki faqih with a very respectable reputation. After almost a year in Tripoli Sidi Ahmad continued onwards to Tunis where he was to study with the renowned Sufi, faqih and hadith expert Abu Abdullah Muhammad ibn Qasim al-Rasa al-Tunisi (d. 894AH). Further in the journey Sidi Ahmad spent some time in Bijayah, the coastal city in modern day Algeria. He spent time writing here (as some of his works attest to) as well as studying with Abul Hasan al-Qalsadi (d. 891AH) another hadith scholar who was also a Sufi and faqih.

Sidi Ahmad Zarruq
Monitor of Scholars and Saints

Sidi Ahmad was to arrive back in Fez in 879AH after some seven years of travel and study and by now his own fame and reputation had grown and had preceded him. A reception of scholars greeted him on arrival but as this story told by Qadi Abu Abdullah al-

27 'He was an imam of the highest rank, a good researcher and author of several books. He was a leading jurist and theologian' al-Makhluf, *Shajarat al-Nur* p.259

Karrasi illustrates Sidi Ahmad's standards of scrupulousness left other scholars behind.

> "When Zarruq returned from the East, the fuqaha of Fez went out to meet him and I was also with them. As soon as we greeted him and sat down in his tent he started asking the fuqaha about the source of their livelihood. Some of them said that most of their livelihood was obtained from endowments (*awqaf al-muhbusa*). The Shaykh [Zarruq] said 'There is no means nor power except by Allah, you feed from dead flesh!' The faqih Ibn Habbak said 'Sire, all praise is for Allah who made us hunt the dead flesh which is allowed by the Shariah by necessity, and did not make us to hunt from live flesh which is forbidden in all circumstances. The Shaykh cried and fell unconscious. Then we went out leaving him alone."

It is clear that for Sidi Ahmad Zarruq – the role of the scholar is to be exemplary in conduct and paramount in that is having lawful income. His life was not just one of learning but rather one of rigorously applying what he had learnt. He was uniquely given the title *muhtasib al-ulama wal-awliya* 'monitor of scholars and saints.'[28]

He was to spend the next few years in Fez, getting married for the first time and was to be blessed with two sons, Ahmad al-Akbar and Ahmad al-Asghar. Although the stay in Fez may not have been an easy for him, he did complete a number of important works in this period including a few commentaries[29] on the *Hikam*

28 'This is a grand and majestic attribute with which no Muslim scholar before or after him has been qualified' Abdullah Kannun, *Mashahir Rijal al-Maghrib* vol.23 p.13

29 Sidi Ahmad was to write more than twenty commentaries on the *Hikam*

of Ibn Ata'Allah al-Iskandari, *Sharh Mabahith al-Asliya, Juz fi Ilm al-Hadith* and the famous *Qawa'id al-Tasawwuf.*

The Journey to Misrata

In 884AH Sidi Ahmad was to leave Fez and head to Cairo stopping in Bijayah on the way, where he was to complete some more of his written works. Further ahead he was to spend over a year in Cairo before making another Hajj journey from there. Visiting Shaykh al-Hadrami was important to Sidi Ahmad as it had been his Shaykh's wish that he travel to Morocco. Reconnecting with Shaykh al-Hadrami was a wonderful experience and Sidi Ahmad was to spend some seven months with him.

In Cairo he was also to spend time with Imam al-Sakhawi again who gave him an *ijazah*. Sidi Ahmad left Cairo and, when he went to say farewell to his Shaykh, the latter wrote some verses of poetry on a piece of paper for him:

"Live unknown among people and be satisfied with it,
This is safer for life and religion
Who mingles with people, his religion will not be safe,
And he will be living between doubt and suspicion"

Following his master's advice Sidi Ahmad, at the age of forty, travelled and eventually settled in Misrata[30] a coastal town in modern day Libya (where it is now the third largest city).

He wrote to Shaykh al-Hadrami on the 22nd of Rajab 886AH:

> "You have known Sire, that I am in Misrata because of what came into my heart that I must obey. We are unable

30 Misrata is some 116 miles east of Tripoli and 513 miles west of Benghazi – the largest and second largest cities in Libya

> to do anything but turn wherever the wind of our destiny turns and accept whatever emanates from it with the help of Allah, since each destiny has been recorded in a book. We do not care where we are, so long as we are numbered among the beloved ones"[31]

Misrata was very welcoming to Sidi Ahmad and he was to become a beloved son of the city and its inhabitants, who would consult him regarding their affairs. Here he took another wife[32] who bore him two more sons and a daughter[33]. His fame spread far and wide and large numbers of students came to study with him. He stayed here for the rest of his life leaving just twice, once to Algiers (in 891AH) and once for a final Hajj journey (in 894AH). During this latter trip he passed through Cairo once again – this time as someone whose reputation had spread far and wide – was welcomed by scholars and princes and taught at the prestigious al-Azhar.[34]

Al-Kuhin mentions:

> "When Shaykh Zarruq arrived in Egypt, the scholars and distinguished people welcomed him and gathered around him and six thousand people from Cairo and its suburbs attended his lectures at al-Azhar al-Sharif. They handed him the leadership of the Maliki school of law and he became the leader of their school. A chair was established for him, and he used to sit there to deliver his lectures. That chair still exists in the *riwaq al-maghribiyah* (living quarters of the students of the Maghrib) at al-Azhar al-Sharif. Shaykh

31 Khusaim p 27
32 A local woman by the name of Amat al-Jalil
33 Ahmad Abu Fath, Ahmad Abul Fadl and Aisha
34 Al-Kuhin, *Tabaqat Shadhiliyah*

> Zarruq had a great influence on the royal family (*umara*) and had acceptance and popularity amongst the masses and the notables[35]."

KARAMAT OF SIDI AHMAD ZARRUQ

By this stage in Sidi Ahmad's life he had travelled widely and studied with the most important scholars in the Muslim world. He had mastered the major sciences of the Shariah and also excelled in Tasawwuf thus he had combined the practice of outward knowledge with the inward knowledge. He had led a sincere and Sunnah inspired life and Allah had blessed him with the peaks of Shariah, Tariqa and Haqiqah. Many *karamat*[36] were reported from many different sources. A few examples are presented by way of illustration:

Abdullah Abu Bakr al-Misrati al-Bilali said "Once I travelled from Fezzan with some companions. I committed myself to the Shaykh [Ahmad Zarruq]. One night I thought it would be wise to leave my companions and sleep somewhere apart from them. I did so. At midnight highwaymen came and robbed them. I fled without food or water or experience of the road. That land is too barren to be known except by an expert guide. All night I heard a voice saying 'Turn right, go left...' till the morning. When I was able to see, I saw a short man walking before me. Whenever I attempted to catch him I found that he went far off, and whenever I missed the right way he shouted at me to follow it again, until I

35 Al-Kuhin, *Tabaqat Shadhiliyah* p19,20

36 Miracles manifested at the hands of the Awliya'Allah – the Friends of Allah – an integral part of Islamic beliefs, see *Aqidah Tahawiyah* 'The Creed of Imam al-Tahawi' translated by Sh. Hamza Yusuf point 124 'We believe in the *karamat*, the miracles of the Awliya as conveyed and verified by trustworthy narrators'

entered Waddan on the third day. I neither felt tired nor thirsty, although it was the summer season!"

Muhammad al-Ayyashi said that once he was travelling with a caravan from Fez to Sudan. The caravan passed through the desert and it was very hot. There was not a single drop of water and the people were under great strain. As soon as they had asked Allah Almighty through Zarruq, a mule appeared carrying waterskins and a man behind it. When he came nearer to them he said "Take the water. Unfortunately you were not in my vicinity so I was a bit late!"

Abu Zakariya al-Bija'i states that he was with Sidi Ahmad Zarruq and other Pilgrims in al-Madina al-Munawara who were depressed as they had no means by which to return home. At midday Sidi Ahmad came to them and said 'Prepare yourselves to set off. I have just come from the Prophet ﷺ who told me to do so.' Unbelievably they began preparing. Suddenly a man came to them and offered them means of travel. While they were bidding their Madani friends farewell another man came running to the she-camel of the Shaykh. He was weeping and saying through his tears "My lord Shihab al-Din! Be my intercessor with Allah! I have just seen the Prophet ﷺ riding his she-camel. When I asked him whether he intends to leave us he said 'No, but I am going to say goodbye to Zarruq!' Everyone burst into tears and that was his last Hajj.

Sidi Ahmad Zarruq's Heritage

He died at the age of 54, may Allah be well pleased with him, in 899AH, and was buried in Misrata. Despite his renown he led a life of *zuhd*, leaving just '...half a mare shared between him and Hajj Abdullah ibn Muhammad al-Dkerani al-Misrati, a white burnus (cape), a woollen *jubbah* and dress, a *misbah* given to him by his master al-Hadrami, and fourteen volumes on different subjects.

His grave was much visited for *barakah* and a *zawiya* and mosque were built in the vicinity.[37]

A final story to illustrate visitation to the maqam of Sidi Ahmad

Muhammad al-Shutaibi states "On my way to North Africa I visited Sidi Ahmad Zarruq's tomb and resolved not to leave unless divine permission came to me. For three years I stayed there seeing the Shaykh in my sleep ordering me to leave. I did not believe the vision until I saw him while I was awake during the daylight with the Prophet ﷺ. He said to me 'O Muhammad! The Prophet bids you go, otherwise you will be deprived. I said ' Yes, Sire, now I will go.' When I was ready to leave he said ' Surely, we will miss you Muhammad!"

His real heritage was thus not the meagre worldly belongings that he left behind but rather the large number students who combined mastery of the outward knowledge as well as inward knowledge who went forth and spread the light of Islam – along with nearly a hundred works on the traditional Islamic sciences that he had mastered and excelled in. The next section will look at Sidi Ahmad Zarruq's works.

The fact that most of the Sufi *silsilas* (continuous initiatic chain going back to the Prophet ﷺ) of the Shadhili Tariqa (the light of which has spread worldwide) have Sidi Ahmad Zarruq in them is no accident.

37 It is noted with sadness that in August 2012 –after the turmoil that Libya has found itself in in recent years that the maqam of Sidi Ahmad Zarruq was desecrated – may Allah illume his resting place.

Works of Sidi Ahmad Zarruq[38]

Sidi Ahmad Zarruq was a prolific writer. His first work was completed in his early twenties and he continued to write until the end of his life. Al-Kuhin calculated, '...that from the time of his birth till his death he wrote half a page a day[39].' He covered a wide range of subjects as the list below shows;

ALCHEMY

1. *Al-Kashf*

AUTOBIOGRAPHY AND BIOGRAPHY

2. *Fihrist*
3. *Al-Kunnash fi Ilm al-Ash*
4. *Manaqib al-Hadrami*

CORRESPONDENCE

5. *Rasa'il li al-salikin*
6. *Risalah ila Abd al-Nabi al-Asfar*
7. *Risalah ila Abd'Allah al-Maghrawi*
8. *Wasiyah*
9. *An al-Wujud*

INVOCATION

10. *Du'a*
11. *Fath al-Maqam al-Asma*
12. *Al-Hafizah*
13. *Minhaj Hizb al-Bahr*
14. *Sharh Asma' Allah al-Husna*
15. *Sharh Dalail al-Khayrat*
16. *Sharh Hizb al-Bahr*
17. *Sharh Hizb al-Barr*
18. *Sharh Mughmadat Hizbai al-Shadhili*

38 Taken from Khushaim, *Zarruq the Sufi* p50-52

39 Al-Kuhin, *Tabaqat al-Shadhiliyah* p.20

19. *Al-Wazifah*

JURISPRUDENCE

20. *Manasik al-Hajj*
21. *Sharh al-Ghafiqiyah*
22. *Sharh al-Hakim al-Tirmidhi*
23. *Sharh al-Irshad*
24. *Sharh Mawadi min Mukhtasar Khalil*
25. *Sharh Nazm al-Riq'i*
26. *Sharh Qawid Iyad*
27. *Sharh al-Qurubiyah*
28. *Sharh Risalat al-Qairawani*
29. *Sharh al-Waghlisiyah*

MEDICINE

30. *Al-Kunnash*
31. *Talkhis al-Durrah al-Muntakhabah*

QURAN

32. *Sharh al-Fatiha*
33. *Tafsir al-Quran*

SCIENCE OF NUMBERS AND LETTERS

34. *Al-Arf fi Ta'rif al-Harf*
35. *Risalah fi al-Add bi al-Asabi*
36. *Sharh al-Siniyah*

SUFISM

37. *Al-Ham fi Sharh Abyat al-Jam*
38. *Fi I'rab in lam ajid ilahi*
39. *Kitab al-I'anat al-Mutawajjih al-Miskin ila al-Fath wa al-Tamkin*
40. *Al-Jami*
41. *Al-Kalam ala anwa ahl al-Khususiyah*
42. *Kitab al-Mahabbah*

43. *Muzil al-Labs*
44. *Al-Nasa'ih*
45. *Al-Nasihah al-Kafiyah*
46. *Al-Nasihah wa haththal-Qarihah*
47. *Al-Nush al-Anfa wa al-Junnah*
48. *Qawaid al-Tasawwuf*
49. *Rawdat al-Azhar*
50. *Risalah*
51. *Risalah fi al-Radd ala Ahl al-Bidah*
52. *Kitab al-Sama*
53. *Sharh Abyat Tatahhar Bima al-Ghaib*
54. *Sharh al-Ajrrumiyah*
55. *Sharh al-Haqa'iq wa al-Daqa'iq*
56. *Sharh al-Mabahith al-Asliyah*
57. *Sharh al-Marasid*
58. *Sharh Muqatta'at al-Shushtari*
59. *Sharh al-Nasihah al-Kafiyah*
60. *Sharh Nuniyyat al-Shushtari*
61. *Sharh al-Sharishiyah*
62. *Sharh Sudur al-Maratib*
63. *Sharh al-Waghlisiyah*
64. *Shuruh al-Hikam*
65. *Suluk al-Tariq idha Fuqida al-Rafiq*
66. *Ta'sis al-Qawaid wa al-Usul*
67. *Tuhfat al-Murid*
68. *Uddat al-Murid al-Sadiq*
69. *Al-Uns*
70. *Urjuzah fi Uyub al-Nafs*
71. *Al-Usul al-Badi 'ah wa al-Jawami al-Rafi'ah*
72. *Usul al-Tariq*

73. *Usul al-Tariqah wa'usus al-Haqiqah*
74. *Wasiyah*
75. *Waraqah fi Ilaj Adwas al-Qalb*

AQIDAH (THEOLOGY)

76. *Sharh Aqidat al-Ghazali*
77. *Sharh al-Murshidah*

TRADITION

78. *Hashiyah ala Muslim*
79. *Juz fi Ilm al-Hadith*
80. *Risalah fi Tahdid Mustalah al-Hadith*
81. *Sharh al-Arba'in Hadithan*
82. *Sharh Hadith 'al-Ma'idatu Baitu al-Da'*
83. *Ta'liq ala al-Bukhari*

TRAVEL

84. *Al-Rihlah*

As well as the above there are ten works on poetry.

Details of Some of the Works of Sidi Ahmad Zarruq[40]

1. *Kitab al-I'anat al-Mutawajjih al-Miskin ila al-Fath wa al-Tamkin* (The Book on Helping the Poor Seeker towards the Path of Victory and Success) is a guide book to the path for a true disciple. The work primarily covers three basic stages of spirituality. According to Sidi Ahmad Zarruq, the first stage of the spiritual sciences is the repentance of misdeeds (*tawbah*) and sincere intention to the Truth while in the second stage a seeker aims to enrich his spiritual states by showing a consistency in the repentance and embellishing his character with high level of morality which takes

40 Taken from *A Critical Edition of Qawaid al-Tasawwuf* by Ghulam Shamas ur Rehman

him to the final stage of realization and gnosis.

2. *Al-Kunnash fi Ilm al-Ash*

(An Anthology on the Science of Anything) is an autobiography of Zarruq which contains some important biographical details of his life, a short introduction to his teachers and their ideas, methods of the Sufi initiation, the Shadhili prayers and amulets, *salawat* blessings on the Prophet ﷺ, Names of Allah, on purity and manners, on the opening of Quranic Surahs and definitions of some Sufi terms. It was written in the last few years of his life when he was over fifty years in age.

3. *Al-Nasihah al-Kafiyah*

(The Sufficient Advice for He Whom Allah has Especially Protected from Evil) is an amalgamation of various topics of jurisprudence, Sufism, and theology. Sidi Ahmad Zarruq presented in this work the details of five foundations of Islamic beliefs. Then he described those prohibited matters which are the basic hindrance in the way of realization of Truth. He also analysed the role of human instincts in the process of acting upon divine commands and the extent to which human instincts can be directed to the Truth and how. There were a number of commentaries written on this including *al-Mawarid al-Safiyah fi Sharh al-Nasihah al-Kafiyah* by Abu Madyan ibn Ahmad ibn Muhammad al-Fasi and *Sharh al-Nasihah al-Kafiyah* by Muhammad ibn Abd al-Rahman ibn Zakri (d.1144AH/1731CE)

4. *Sharh Aqidat al-Ghazali*

(A Commentary on the *Aqidah* al-Imam al-Ghazali): al-Ghazli composed a commentary, *al-Risalah al-Qudsiyah,* on his own theological work, *Qawa'id al-I'tiqad*. Later he included both these works as a chapter, *Kitab Qawa'id al-Aqa'id,* in his famous book *Ihya Ulum al-Din*. Zarruq interpreted Ghazali's theological thoughts on the issue of Divine Oneness and His attributes, prophecy, Islamic eschatology and the intercession of the Prophet in the light of Sunni Ashari scholars, evoking Sufi wisdom in the process.

5. *Sharh al-Mabahith al-Asliyah li-Ibn al-Banna*

(A Commentary on the Original Discussions of Ibn al-Banna) is the most celebrated poetical work of Abu al-Abbas ibn Banna al-Saraqusti, a leading Sufi of the Maghrib (d. 649AH/1251CE). It consists of 473 verses and is divided into five sections. Sidi Ahmad Zarruq explained and interpreted the Sufi thought of Ibn al-Banna in light of the framework of the Shadhili masters.

6. *Sharh al-Qurtubiyah*

(A Commentary on *al-Qurtubiyah*) is a commentary on the famous book of Maliki jurisprudence *Urjuzah al-Wildan* written by Sadiq al-Din Abu Bakr Yahya ibn Umar al-Azdi al-Qurtubi (d. 567AH/1171CE).

7. *Sharh Risalah al-Qayrawani*

(A Commentary on *Risalah al-Qayrawani*) is a commentary on a famous book of Maliki jurisprudence, *al-Risalah* of Abdullah ibn Abi Zayd al-Qayrawani (d. 389AH/999CE). Zarruq extensively explained all the contents of this book regarding Islamic rites, rules of conduct, and Islamic penal and family law according to the Maliki school of law. He also discussed indirectly some theological debates in the prolegomena in the light of the Ashari school of Aqidah (theology).

8. *Sharh al-Hikam*

(A commentary on *al-Hikam*) is a commentary on one of the most important works of Sufism by Taj al-Din Ibn Ata'Allah al-Iskandari. *Al-Hikam* is written in an aphoristic style and contains profound meanings and wisdom. Several commentaries have been written on it by renowned scholars. The book had a special place in the heart of Sidi Ahmad Zarruq as his biographers record that he composed more than twenty commentaries on it.

9. *Uddat al-Murid al-Sadiq*

(The Equipment of a True Novice) revolves around the concept of *bid'ah* (reprehensible innovation). Defining and classifying *bid'ah*, Sidi Ahmad formulated 100 sections focusing on the issue of *bid'ah* in order to avoid it in all theological, jurisprudential and spiritual matters. Putting emphasis on the sunnah, he advised a true novice to refrain from all kinds of religious innovations.

10. *Ta'liq ala al-Bukhari*

(A commentary on al-Bukhari) is a commentary on *al-Jami' al-Sahih* of Imam Abu Muhammad Ismail al-Bukhari (d. 256AH/870CE) in the field of hadith. Sidi Ahmad Zarruq described the historical significance of the Prophetic reports and explained the difficult words and complexities of the text. Moreover he also evaluated the *isnads* of some hadiths.

11. *Qawa'id al-Tasawwuf*

(Principles of Sufism) is the subject of a number of studies and has been translated, the best study of it do date has been the work of Ghulam Shamas ur Rehman *A Critical Edition of Qawaid al-Tasawwuf.*

About *Hizb al-Bahr*

In a hadith the Prophet said 'Prayer is the essence of worship[41]'. The Shadhilis were at the forefront in following the Prophetic example when it came to invocations as Shaykh Nuh Keller notes[42]:

> 'Because it was part of the Prophet's tremendous nature (Allah bless him and give him peace) to continually make remembrance at all times, and to persevere in the good works he had at hand, he was followed in this by the pious early Muslims and those who came after, of the friends of the All-merciful, who in addition to sunna invocations and reciting the Koran, made their times flourish with remembrances and litanies, of the very soul of the Koran and sunna, resplendent in eloquence, majestic in form, and joining in meaning between knowledge, conduct and gnosis. Among the greatest of these litanies and most comprehensive were those of the sheikh of the path , the Imam of spiritual reality, and beacon of Sacred Law, my master Abul Hasan al-Shadhili (Allah be well pleased with him) and the scholars of religious excellence who

41 At-Tirmidhi and Musnad Imam Ahmad
42 Shaykh Nuh Keller, *Invocations of the Shadhili Order p3-4*

followed in his footsteps, the spiritual graces (*barakat*) of whose invocations have encompassed both the elite of the Muslims and the common, to hear of which not like seeing.'

The *Hizb al-Bahr* itself consists mostly of Quranic verses and Prophetic invocations to be found in the various authentic collection of hadith. It is clear that it has found acceptance in the Ummah due to huge popularity that it has achieved. But the Shadhili shaykhs are keen to point out that the *Hizb al-Bahr*

'Is not a magic wand, but an expression of slavehood and poverty[43]'

So how did this invocation come about? Ibn al-Sabbagh has the story in his *Durrat al-Asrar* a translation of which is in the next section.

The Story of the Origin of the Blessed Prayer Known as the *Hizb al-Bahr* Litany of the Sea[44]

The righteous Shaykh Abū al-ʿAzāʾim Māḍī ibn Sulṭān[45] (may Allah have mercy on him) told us in the city of Tunis (may Allah watch over it), as did the righteous and blessed Shaykh Sharaf al-Dīn, the Shaykh's son, in the city of Damanhūr al-Waḥsh[46] in Egypt, in the year 715 AH:

The Shaykh [Abul Hasan al-Shadhili] decided to set out from Cairo to perform the pilgrimage, a little while after the main pilgrimage party had set out. He said, 'I have been commanded to perform the pilgrimage this year, so find me a vessel on the

---

43 Shaykh Nuh Keller, *Sea Without Shore* p176
44 From Ibn al-Ṣabbāgh's *Durrat al-Asrār* p50-51
45 This was Sidi Abul Hasan's servant
46 Ancient city some hundred miles northwest of Cairo

Nile[47] to take me across Upper Egypt[48].' They searched for a vessel and found only a ship belonging to Christians on which was an elderly Christian man and his sons. He said, 'We shall board it.' So we boarded it and set out from Cairo. After two or three days the wind changed so that it was blowing against us, so we made berth on the Nile shore in an uninhabited place. We remained there for around a week, the hills of Cairo still within our sights. One of the pilgrims with us said, 'How could the Shaykh say he was commanded to perform the pilgrimage this year, when it is already too late? When is this journey going to end?'

The Shaykh slept through the middle of the day, and then rose and recited this Litany. Then he asked for the captain of the ship, and asked him his name. He said his name was Mismār. The Shaykh said, 'O blessed Mismar, unfurl the sails.' He said, 'Are we going back to Cairo, sir?' He replied, 'We are continuing on our way, Allah willing.' The captain said, 'This wind will only bear us back to Cairo before the day is out, and in any case is too strong to sail in.' The Shaykh said, 'Unfurl the sails with the blessing of Allah.'

So we opened the sails, and Allah commanded the wind to change, and the sails were filled so suddenly that the crew had no time to untie the rope from the stake and had to chop it off instead; and we set off with a goodly wind. The captain and his brother announced that they had embraced Islam. Their father began to weep, saying, 'I have lost my sons on this voyage!' The

47 The journey by boat on the Nile was preferable to travelling by land where highwaymen and bandits would often lie in wait for pilgrims.

48 The Nile is one of the few rivers that flows northwards. To go on Hajj, pilgrims would go by boat against the flow of the river (thus relying on strong winds) heading to the south (Upper Egypt) to Qena. From Qena they would travel to Marsa Alam from where they would cross the Red Sea to Jeddah and then onwards to Mecca.

Shaykh said to him, 'Nay, you have gained them.'

That night, the elderly Christian man dreamed it was the Day of Resurrection. He saw Paradise and Hell, and saw the Shaykh leading a great throng into Paradise, his sons among them. He wanted to follow them, but was not allowed to do so, and a voice said to him, 'You are not one of them until you enter their religion.' He told the Shaykh about this dream and embraced Islam. The Shaykh said to him, 'The people you saw with me are my followers until the Day of Resurrection.'

We travelled on, and the journey was made easy for us by many events which would be long in the telling, and all of us performed the pilgrimage that year.

Sidi Māḍī (may Allah have mercy on him) added: The elderly Christian man became a great Friend of Allah. He sold his ship and performed the pilgrimage with us along with his sons, and established a zāwiya in Upper Egypt. Many miracles were granted to him, and this journey itself was one of them. May Allah have mercy on him, and be well pleased with him.

The Shaykh رضي الله عنه said, 'By Allah, I received [this Litany] from none other than the Messenger of Allah ﷺ, who dictated it to me directly. He said to me, "Guard it, for it contains the Supreme Name of Allah." Wherever it is recited, there is security. Had the people of Baghdad known it, the Tartars would not have taken the city.'

Recitation of the *Hizb al-Bahr*

Hizb al-Bahr's acceptance in the Ummah is clear from the multitudes of people that recite it daily worldwide, and derive immense benefit from it.

It is related from Ibn Ayyad[49] that:

> "Shaykh 'Abd al-Raḥmān al-Bisṭāmī said about the Litany of the Sea, 'It has spread out in the land and become renowned and esteemed, and has been recited in many mosques and proclaimed in all kinds of places.' The scholars have said that it contains the Supreme Name and the Great Universal Secret, to the point where it is related that Shaykh Abū al-Ḥasan al-Shādhilī himself said, 'Had my Litany been invoked in Baghdad, it would not have been conquered.' It is the ample provision and the invincible shield, and through it all woes can be relieved by the subtlest unseen means. Wherever it is recited, that place is safe from blights and protected from calamities. To beginners on the spiritual path it gives curative secrets, and to those at the end of the path it gives dazzling illuminations. Whoever invokes it every day after sunrise, Allah hears his call, relieves his distress, raises his rank among the people, expands his breast with knowledge of the divine Oneness, gives him ease in his affairs, lightens his difficulties, protects him from the evil of men and jinn, and keeps him safe from the mishaps of night and day. Anyone who looks upon him will love him. If he recites it in the presence of a tyrant, he will be safe from his evil. Whoever invokes it after every prayer, Allah Almighty enriches him from having need for His creatures, keeps him safe from the vicissitudes of time, and eases him towards happiness in every movement and rest. Whoever invokes it in the first hour of Friday, Allah

49 Ibn Ayyad, *al-Mafākhir al-'Aliyya*, page 185-186

puts love for him in the hearts of the people. One scholar said that whoever writes it on something, that thing will be protected by Allah's power and might. Whoever continues to recite it regularly will not die by choking, drowning, burning or being struck by lightning. If the wind fails for people in a ship and they invoke it, a goodly wind will come to them, by Allah's leave. Whoever writes it on the wall of a city or house, Allah will protect that city or house from the evil of sudden mishaps and blights. It has powerful benefits at times of war. It is a prayer of succour and victory against all foes, whether jinn or men. We have only briefly touched upon its benefits here, and may Allah bless the one who said:

> Invoke the Litany of the Sea and it will show you wonders,
> Give you ease in your affairs, and lend you strength.
> You will find the sea obedient and the wind submissive;
> You will find gentleness quickly, and your time will be joyful."

It is recited individually as well as in a group, for general benefit or for specific aims – a number of scholarly works have been penned mentioning the *fawa'id* or benefits. These works are popular throughout the Muslim world but prove particularly popular in the Indian sub-continent where many have written works listing the means by which *Hizb al-Bahr* can be recited to achieve a particular aim. Shah Abd al-Aziz Muhaddith Delhvi (d.1823CE) wrote one such work and his father Shah Waliullah wrote a full commentary on the *Hizb al-Bahr* (see below).

The following advice is found in *Sea Without Shore – A Manual of the Sufi Path;'*

Hizb al-Bahr or 'The Litany of the Sea' is recited after the mid-afternoon prayer (*'asr*). Some read it at sunrise, at which time it possesses particular properties, and it is also read whenever one is in particular need of something, in which case one makes one's intention at the words *wa sakhkhir lana hadha l-bahr* ("and subject to us this sea"). Like all of the *hizbs* of the *tariqa*, it should be memorized and recited from one's heart as if it were one's own words, with complete attention to whom one is addressing it. It is not a magic wand, but an expression of slavehood and poverty. In a general way, the purpose of these *wirds* is not only to train the heart in *du'a'*, but to eventually eliminate one's absentmindedness from Allah, and one must strive in them to have presence of heart. Though memorized, they are not rote[50].

COMMENTARIES ON *HIZB AL-BAHR*

Aside from the popular reading among the masses, the *Hizb al-Bahr* also received keen interest from Muslim scholars who have focused their attention and written commentaries on it. Below is a list of just ten such commentaries – it is interesting to note that the commentators come from all the different Sunni schools of law and encompass the whole of the Muslim world from Turkey to India, to various parts of Africa. Many of them were experts in hadith as well.

Dawud ibn Umar ibn Bakhili (d.733AH/1332CE) *al-Latifa al-*

50 Shaykh Nuh Keller, *Sea Without Shore p176*

Mardiya

Abul Huda Muhammad al-Rifa'i (d. 728AH/1328) *Qiladat al-Nahr fi Sharh Hizb al-Bahr*

Ibn Duqmaq (d. 809AH)/1406CE) *Qatf al-Zahr min Sharh Hizb al-Bahr*

Shah Waliullah (d.1114AH/1703CE) *Hawami Sharh Hizb al-Bahr* (Persian)

Abu al-Iqbal Hasan ibn Ali ibn Ahmad al-Mintawi al-Azhari al-Madabighi (d. 1170AH/1756CE) *Sharh Hizb al-Bahr*

Ahmad ibn Umar ibn Ayub al-Izmiri (d. 1180AH/1766) *Fath al-Ali al-Barr Sharh Hizb al-Bahr*

Mustafa al-Kamali (d. 1210AH/1795CE) *Jannat al-Nasr Fi Khawas Hizb al-Bahr*

Muhammad Bello ibn Usman dan Fodio (d.1253AH/1837CE) *Sharh Hizb al-Bahr*

Haji Imdadullah Muhajir Makki (d.1317AH/1899CE) *Hizb al-Bahr*

Yusuf Nabhani (d.1350AH/1932CE) *Sharh Hizb al-Bahr*

Sidi Ahmad Zarruq's *Sharh Hizb al-Bahr*

But by far and wide the most widely respected commentary on the *Hizb al-Bahr* is Sidi Ahmad Zarruqs of which there are various editions available. This translation is based on an edition that has taken considerable time to compile from the original manuscripts and it is due to be published in the Arabic by Dar al-Fath Research and Publications of Amman, Jordan. The edition is considerably longer than many of the easily available online versions which are often missing significant sections of Sidi Ahmad's Introduction and Conclusion.

Introduction

In the Name of Allah, the Compassionate, the Merciful
Blessings and peace be upon our master Muḥammad and his Family and Companions.

THE SHAYKH AND IMAM, the righteous guide, Sidi Abū al-ʿAbbās Aḥmad ibn Aḥmad ibn Muḥammad ibn ʿĪsā al-Burnusī Zarrūq al-Fāsī (may Allah have mercy on him and be well pleased with him) says:

Praise be to Allah, who guided His saints to the paths of intermediaries to Him, and channelled all manner of graces through their hands, so that he who follows them is given aid and guidance, while he who strays from their path gets lost and wanders blindly; and he who grasps the hems of their garments finds success and good fortune, while he who rejects them is cut off and ruined. I praise Him as one who knows that there is no refuge from Him save with Him. I thank Him as one who is certain that the goodness of this world and the world to come is in His hands. I seek His aid as one who relies on no one but Him in all things. I ask His forgiveness as one who flees from his sins to Him. I ask for His goodness as one who knows that the goodness of all things is with Him. And I invoke blessings and peace upon our master Muḥammad and his Family and Companions, as plentiful as the creations of Allah the Generous and all His graces.

I would like to present a simple treatise serving as a commentary on the protective litany [*ḥafīẓa*] known as the *Ḥizb al-Baḥr*, attributed to the shaykh, imam, scholar and spiritual authority, our master, liege and intermediary to our Lord, Shaykh Abū al-Ḥasan ʿAlī ibn ʿAbd al-Jabbār al-Ḥasanī al-Shādhilī, who is well known for his virtues and feats and for being the perfected Pole [*quṭb*] and realised saint. We have done this in hope of sharing in his blessing and his favour, and seeking his benefit, goodwill and virtue. We depend on Allah alone in completing this task, for He is our sufficiency and the best of patrons.

I say, then – and all aid comes from Allah, and on Him we depend – that it is necessary for us first to present some introductory chapters, and later some concluding chapters. As for the introduction, it will contain three chapters:

- The first concerns the nature of litanies [*aḥzāb*] and their purpose, their rules, and the reasons why they may be rejected or accepted;
- The second concerns the requirements for composing a litany and using it, the proper intention of the one who composes it and the one who uses it, and the ruling of this and matters adjacent to it;
- The third concerns the reason why this litany is called the 'Litany of the Sea', why it was composed, how it should be used, the rulings of travel by sea and the special qualities of the sea.

As for the Conclusion, it will also have three parts, which are all concerned with the rulings about imitation [*tashabbuh*] and how and why it should be done. Let us without further ado begin the introduction.

INTRODUCTION – PART ONE

The reality of litanies and their purpose, rules, and related matters

A litany is a regular invocation [*wird*] used for the purpose of worship and the like. Its technical definition is: *a group of invocations, supplications and prayers composed for the purpose of remembrance, reminding, taking refuge from evil, requesting goodness, seeking knowledge, and above all directing the heart to Allah Almighty in all this.* Litanies as such did not exist in the first generation nor those who followed shortly after them, but they began to appear on the tongues of Sufi shaykhs and righteous folk of the Muslim community for the purpose of guiding them to focus in the right place and encourage the idle to work, help the disciples, strengthen the lovers, safeguard the initiates, raise the aspirations of the worshippers, ascetics and people of piety and steadfastness, and to open the door for the masses of believers to enter. They did this because they saw how aspirations had waned, resolves weakened, intentions faded and dispositions diminished, and how heedlessness had ascended, hearts grown sick and certitude grown faint.

Now some of these folk followed the way of compilation and

arrangement, compiling the hadiths related about invocations for morning and evening, and the different phrases of praise, glorification and lauding of Allah as given verbatim in the primary texts without adding anything to them. They did this in order to stay on the safe side and adhere rigidly to the outer form, which was safer.

Then there were others who followed the way of adding new things, which was wiser and more complete, especially when they avoided troublesome and ambiguous elements in their invocations and supplications; one of them was Shaykh Abū al-Ḥasan ﵁, who received them by way of divine inspiration and took them from their Source [the Prophet ﷺ] both in dreams and in waking visions, and this was more complete still. This group was the best of all of them in state, the soundest in intention, and the firmest in speech.

Then there were those who took the position of gnosis and knowledge, caring not whether what they said was ambiguous or difficult; one of them was Shaykh Abū Muḥammad ʿAbd al-Ḥaqq ibn Sabʿīn, who came up with astounding expressions and verbose, troublesome phrases. This was either because he was simply giving expression to his spiritual state, which seems likely, or because he intended them to be for the spiritual elites only, who would not be troubled by them, which is also likely. Thus they should be avoided by the weak, and even the strong should pass over them without criticism as long as there is any possibility that they can be interpreted in a way that accords with the truth, and reasonable arguments and excuses can be offered for them. The truth speaks clearly, while falsehood stammers. Let he who recognises them follow them, and he who is ignorant of them pass over them in silence. Criticism is worthless, and making excuses without having the right to is plain error.

Now you might say, 'People have said terrible things about Ibn Sabʿīn which make it necessary that he be disregarded, so why should any attention be paid to his knowledge, supplications or invocations?' We answer that no statement should be accepted without proof, nor should anything be taken without justification. It has been affirmed that he was a man of knowledge, and related that he was a man of spiritual insights and states – indeed, this has been confirmed by many great men who came after him. Therefore no heed should be paid to the criticism of those who seek to diminish his rank, and none of his teachings should be taken except those whose status is clear. The same goes for all of those who follow his way. If knowledge is sacred, then the people of knowledge are also sacred; the believer makes excuses, while the hypocrite looks for faults and even relates them to others without any right. No one is more ignorant than a partisan of falsehood or someone who criticises what he does not understand. Know that speech is an attribute of the speaker, and that what you say will show what you are. The one who is quick to criticise is no different from the one who is quick to be duped. The one who has the most right to the truth is the one who makes the effort to seek it out, and even takes difficult and dangerous stances if that is what it takes to find guidance, and if it does not go against what is required of him; and all success is with Allah.

In sum, the litanies of the masters are descriptions of their states, and pearls of their speech and legacies of their knowledge and deeds. They did not follow caprice in anything they did, which is why their speech has been accepted. Now perhaps there came after them people who wanted to imitate this solely for their own personal ends, and thus what they did ended up producing the opposite of the desired effect. It is like the story of the bee who taught the hornet how to make a hive, so the hornet set about making one, and when it was done she said, 'Now I am just as good as the bee!' The bee replied, 'There is the hive, but where is the honey?' What matters is not the house, but the occupant.

The litanies of the folk of perfection are bound up with their spiritual states, aided by their knowledge, bolstered by their inspiration and accompanied by their miracles. Shaykh Abū al-Ḥasan ﷺ himself said about al-Ḥizb al-Kabīr ['the Great Litany'], 'He who reads it will have what we have, and there will be upon him what is upon us.' Sidi Abū 'Abdallāh Muḥammad ibn 'Abbād[51] (may Allah have mercy on him) said, 'What he meant is, "He will have the sanctity we have, and the mercy that is on us."' I say that the strength of the speech indicates that this is a declaration that such a person enters the inner circle of the Shaykh in a way that covers more than just sanctity and mercy. Now this applies to all his litanies and his *ṭarīqa* entirely, because if only to believe in the *ṭarīqa* of the Sufis is sainthood [*wilāya*], then what of entering it even in the slightest? Of course no one would use their litanies unless he loved them, and a man shall be resurrected alongside those he loves, as the Prophet ﷺ said. He also said to the man who asked him about a person who loves people but never had the chance to meet them, *'You will be with those you love.'*[52] May Allah have mercy on Shaykh Abū 'Abdallāh Muḥammad ibn 'Alī al-Tirmidhī al-Ḥakīm, who said, 'O Allah, we seek an intermediary to You through our love of them, for they loved You, and they could not have loved You had You not loved them first; by Your love for them, they attained Your love. We could not have attained love of

51 A famous Sufi born in Ronda, Malaga, Spain, he was a disciple of Ibn 'Āshir and most famous for his commentary on the *Ḥikam* of Ibn 'Aṭā'illāh.

52 Narrated by al-Bukhārī (*Ṣaḥīḥ, al-Aḥkām*, 267).

them for Your sake had we not been given a share of Your love; so complete this for us, until we meet You.' Someone composed these lines on this:

> I know of those who, by their rank,
>   Stand high above the brows of men.
> Though I may not be one of these,
>   I have esteem through loving them.

Know that the litanies of the Shaykh have a great many functions: they impart knowledge and teach the proper conduct of supplication. They are definitions of the spiritual path, beacons guiding to reality and invocations of Allah's glory, grandeur and magnificence. They contain acknowledgments of the soul's baseness and lowliness, warnings against its deceptions and dangers, indications of the nature of the world and creation and the way to flee from them, and reminders of sins and flaws and how to rid oneself of them. They are also guides to the purest and deepest expression of *tawḥīd*, and how to follow the Sacred Law and its requirements. Thus they are teachings in the form of supplications, and supplications in the form of teachings. He who approaches them from the perspective of knowledge will find it within them. He who approaches them from the perspective of action will find this to be their true nature. He who approaches them from the perspective of the spiritual state will find it within them. This has been attested to by the elites and the masses. Anyone who hears any part of them will find that they have an effect on his soul, and will experience the same thing when he reads them himself, unless he is busy with a pressing matter, distracted by a worldly affair or disguising himself behind a false claim – may Allah save us from tribulation!

You might say, 'That is apparent in the Great Litany, but not in the Lesser Litany [i.e. the Litany of the Sea] we are presently discussing.' To this, I say that every individual litany had its own reason for being made, and has its own special properties. Those who reflect on this will find it to be true. We will allude to some of this later, Allah willing.

QUESTION: Taqī al-Dīn ibn Taymiyya criticised these litanies and rejected them vehemently. How can this be answered?

ANSWER: Ibn Taymiyya is acknowledged to have been a great memoriser of hadith, but was criticised on doctrinal grounds and marred by a deficiency of intelligence, never mind gnosis. Shaykh Imam Taqī al-Dīn al-Subkī was asked about him and answered, 'A man whose learning exceeded his intelligence.' This means that attention ought to be paid to his transmissions, but not to his intellectual musings; and Allah knows best.

QUESTION: You have explained the nature and wisdom of litanies; now what of their ruling?

ANSWER: The ruling of litanies is that they are deemed permissible by several Sufis and many scholars, on the grounds that they are a means to worship, and nothing in the Sacred Law indicates that they are not permitted; indeed, there is evidence that they *are* permitted in individual instances, though there is nothing related about the issue on the general level. Ibn al-Ḥājj discussed this matter in *al-Madkhal* in relation to the virtue of invoking after the dawn prayer and noted two opinions: al-Shāfiʿī deemed it permitted [*jāʾiz*], and Mālik deemed it disliked [*makrūh*]. The former supported his opinion with the words of the Prophet ﷺ *'What I have been silent on is excused for you.'*[53] He was

53 Resembles a saying of Ibn ʿAbbās narrated by Abū Dāwūd (*Sunan, al-Aṭʿima,* 3306).

informed about the things his community would do after him, but never made any kind of warning about this. Moreover, litanies are of the type of action which he encouraged.

The basis of the contrary opinion is that if the early Muslims [*salaf*] did not do something, there is no good in it, because they were eager for all that is good and knew the Sunna best. However, the people of all lands in current and recent times consider it to be appropriate today, basing this on the Sufi principle concerning those things that concentrate people's hearts on their Lord: Junayd (may Allah have mercy on him) was asked about spiritual audition [*samāʿ*] and said, 'Everything that concentrates the servant on his Lord is permitted.' Abū ʿAlī al-Daqqāq (may Allah have mercy on him) was asked the same question, and gave the same answer, attributing it to the masters. Qushayrī related this towards the end of his chapter on *samāʿ* in *al-Risāla*.

When Shaykh Abū ʿAbdallāh ibn ʿAbbād (may Allah have mercy on him) spoke in his *Rasāʾil* about regular litanies and how it is related that Mālik disliked using them, he said, 'This is only disliked in times when the people are already firmly adherent to the Sunna and so on; as for today, it should be retained because it is one of the most attractive elements of the religion and if it is lost, its effects will be lost forever.' That is the gist of what he said, and it is a good explanation with many general applications, so reflect on it. There are also hadiths that support this concept.

Now when it comes to the contents of these litanies, whether invocations or the like, there are three forms that they might take:

Firstly, they might contain artifice and flowery language. This is forbidden by the Sacred Law. The Prophet ﷺ forbade that supplications be made to rhyme, so what about other forms of invocation? He also forbade supplications that contain words of aggression against anyone.

Secondly, they might not contain this kind of language, but be full of troublesome and ambiguous language that is not sanctioned by the outward teachings of the Sacred Law, although it might have a hidden meaning that is valid. This is forbidden for the masses, although it might be permitted for the elites if it arises from a spiritual state or the like. This is out of proper etiquette with Allah and to safeguard the doctrine of the weak.

Thirdly, they might be free of both these things and contain quotes from the Qur'an and Sunna or allusions to them. There is a difference of opinion about these instances when they are not verbatim quotations. This is something that the Shādhilīs have been criticised for; the response to it is that this was done under the guidance of true inspiration or a direct meeting in a dream, and inspiration can be acted upon as long as it does not contradict wisdom, change a ruling or establish any new rulings. This is supported by the Prophet's ﷺ words *'In every community there have been those who are spoken to; if they are in my community, 'Umar is one of them'*,[54] and his ﷺ words *'A righteous vision from a righteous man is one forty-sixth of prophethood.'* Another narration adds, *'and what is from prophethood does not lie.'*[55] The litanies of our master [al-Shādhilī] ؓ are certainly from one of these two kinds, and he ؓ himself stated that he did not compose a single letter of them without the permission of Allah and His Messenger. He said (may Allah be well pleased with him), 'Anyone who calls to Allah with something that the Messenger of Allah ﷺ did not, is an innovator.'

Now this 'permission' to which he was alluding could refer to a vision in a dream, or to the legal aspect inasmuch as the

54 Narrated by al-Bukhārī (*Ṣaḥīḥ, al-Anbiyā'*, 3210).
55 Narrated by al-Bukhārī (*Ṣaḥīḥ, al-Ta'bīr*, 6499).

litany only contains what the Sacred Law has permitted, or to permission given during a spiritual state via inspiration. The first of these is the most likely, given that the second implies no special distinction. The third is even better, given that it is implied by the existence of the spiritual path [*ṭarīqa*] itself; however, this is on condition that it accord with the second in a reasonable way, so that the reality [*ḥaqīqa*] and Sacred Law [*sharīʿa*] are combined. If this is then further supported by a vision in a dream, then so much the better. It is most likely that the Shaykh combined all three; and Allah knows best.

QUESTION: The Shaykh often says, 'I was told such-and-such.' What does this mean?

ANSWER: This is the meaning of inspiration [*ilhām*]; something occurs to the soul that cannot be denied or rebutted, nor is it the province of personal caprice. The breast is cooled by it, and the heart expanded, and it flows through the inner being in a way that makes its reality understood. It requires no external proof, and at the same time it accords with the principles of the Law and pertains to something that the Law permits or encourages. This is the meaning of 'being spoken to' [*al-mukālama*] in the language of the Sufis. Shaykh Abū Muḥammad al-Marjānī رضي الله عنه said, 'Anyone who thinks that Allah speaks to people after the prophets in the same way He spoke to Moses عليه السلام, has gone astray in his understanding,' or something along those lines. He continued: 'On the contrary, the Sufis understand Allah's speech as being discourse addressed to their innermost subtle being, that part of them that cannot be assailed by error or penetrated by doubt or misgivings because of the attestation of their spiritual states and their constant experience; and it always accords with the principles of the Law; and Allah knows best.'

OBJECTION: It is related that the righteous shaykh and jurist Abū ʿAbdallāh Muḥammad ibn ʿArafa al-Tūnusī ﷺ said, 'Nothing weighs more heavily on me than the claim of some that "It was said to me". I would not accept this from anyone, even al-Marjānī, who was unquestionably a saint.'

RESPONSE: The reason this weighed heavily on him was that it was not something he was personally experienced with, and that he had witnessed many bad things done by people falsely claiming it; moreover, the outward appearance of the expression is indeed troublesome. Nevertheless, that it weighed heavily on him does not in itself prove anything, since it contains no evidence or rational arguments. Likewise, the fact that he refused to accept it does not do any harm, nor did he harm himself by restricting himself to this, or by rejecting this phenomenon according to his own knowledge. Yet this has no bearing on anyone other than him, for Allah's decree is that no one should go beyond the limits of their own knowledge: ﴿*Do not pursue that of which you have no knowledge*﴾ [17:36].

As for his statement that al-Marjānī was unquestionably a saint, if he came to this conclusion rationally, then reason has no part to play therein. If he based it on textual evidence, then there is no direct textual evidence for it. If he based it on attestations, then attestations of spiritual states cannot yield unquestionable knowledge. If he based it on the consensus of his time, then this cannot amount to unquestionable knowledge today because this consensus has not been mass-transmitted. Moreover, he was not any more famous than other luminaries of his time. If he based it on his fame and renown, then others are even more famous than him; indeed, al-Shādhilī himself certainly had a more profound and powerful impact on the souls of all, both the masses and the elites, as did al-Jīlānī ﷺ, to the extent that ʿIzz al-Dīn ibn

ʿAbd al-Salām said, 'No saint's miracles have reached a greater level of unquestionable knowledge and mass-transmission than the miracles of Shaykh ʿAbd al-Qādir ﷺ.' As for the question of bolstering the spiritual path and being granted perfect guidance, all of them were given guidance and manifest proofs by their Lord, as is attested to by their stories and proven by the impacts they have had; and all success comes from Allah.

QUESTION: What proof do you have that it is permitted to make use of the invocations and litanies composed under inspiration, and what evidence is there that they have any special value?

ANSWER: The proof for this is the direct attestation of the Sunna, and the prophetic hadiths wherein he ﷺ approved of the invocations and supplications he heard from many people at different times, each with distinct wordings and clear meanings, and praised them and encouraged that they be used. They did this even though he ﷺ had not taught them these specific words – for he had taught them the concepts behind them, so that they knew how to compose them correctly.

One example of this is found in the hadith of ʿAbdallāh ibn Burayda, who related on the authority of his father ﷺ that the Prophet ﷺ heard a man say, 'O Allah, I ask You by virtue of my testimony that You are Allah, and there is no god besides You, and You are the One, the Eternally Besought and Self-Sufficient, who neither begets nor is begotten, and who has no equal.' He ﷺ said, *'He has asked Allah by His Supreme Name by which if He is called, He answers, and if He is asked, He gives.'* This was narrated by Abū Dāwūd and al-Tirmidhī, who declared it sound [*ḥasan*]. Ibn Ḥibbān and al-Ḥākim declared it authentic [*ṣaḥīḥ*], and the latter said, 'It is authentic according to the criteria of Muslim.'

Another example is found in the hadith of Muʿādh ibn Jabal ﷺ, who related that the Prophet ﷺ heard a man say, 'O Lord of Majesty and Bounty!' He said, *'You have been answered, so ask and you will be given.'* This was narrated by al-Tirmidhī who said, 'It is a sound hadith.'

Then there is the hadith of Anas ؓ, who reported that the Prophet ﷺ passed by Abū ʿAyyāsh al-Zuraqī as he was praying and heard him say, 'O Allah, I ask You by Your own praiseworthiness, O You besides whom there is no god, O Loving One, O Generous One, O Maker of Heaven and Earth, O Living One, O All-Sustaining One, O Lord of Majesty and Bounty!' He said, *'He has called upon Allah with His Supreme Name by which if He is called, He answers.'* This was narrated by Abū Dāwūd and Ibn Ḥibbān, and by al-Naṣāʾī in his *Ṣaḥīḥ*. Al-Ḥākim said, 'It meets the criteria of Muslim.'

Then there is the hadith of Abū Hurayra ؓ and Abū Ayyūb ؓ about how he was looking after the zakat funds and found a jinn stealing from it, and the jinn pleaded to him so he let it go. This was repeated several times until at last he said to it, 'I will not let you go until I have taken you to the Messenger of Allah ﷺ.' The jinn said, 'I shall tell you something that, if you read it in your house, nothing will be able to come near you, not a demon or anything else.' He said, 'We were very keen to learn good things.' So the jinn told him to read the *Āyat al-Kursī*. This was narrated by al-Bukhārī and others; it is too long to give in full here.

There is also the hadith of Abū Saʿīd ؓ and how he recited the *Fātiḥa* to cure someone who had been stung by an animal, and how the Prophet ﷺ approved of this and did not criticise him for it.[56]

There are so many narrations like this about invocation and prayers of this sort that clearly prove it is permitted, to the extent that this cannot be rebutted. They constitute primary textual

56 See hadith narrated by al-Bukhārī (*Ṣaḥīḥ, al-Ṭibb*, 5736).

proof of this principle; and Allah knows best.

In addition to this, Mālik ☙ included in the chapter on supplication in the *Muwaṭṭa* the words of Abū al-Dardā' upon waking 'The eyes have slept, and the eyelids have taken their rest, and all that remains is You, O Living One, O All-Sustaining One!' If it be objected that this must originally have been the words of the Prophet ﷺ because Abū al-Dardā' would not say something like this unless he had heard it, I say that the principle established above says otherwise, and there is no contradiction between the principle and the outward meaning of this text. Therefore this text is another support for our position; and Allah knows best.

INTRODUCTION – PART TWO

The requirements for composing a litany and using it, and the proper intention of the one who composes it and the one who uses it, and the ruling of this and matters adjacent to it

There are three requirements for composing a litany:

[1] The first is that it flow from the present spiritual state and not from caprice or wilful artifice.

[2] The second is that its wording be free from troublesome, ambiguous and problematic phrases, such that it agrees with the words used by the Lawgiver and their meanings, and that it clearly refers back to the principles established by them.

[3] The third is that it be devoted to Allah alone, and not done in order to win followers, make oneself prominent or show off. All speech is accompanied by the spiritual state of the speaker: if it comes from caprice, it will breed caprice. He who speaks from guidance will guide others with his speech; otherwise, he will not. It was said to Ḥamdūn al-Qaṣṣār (may Allah have mercy on him), 'Why was the speech of the early Muslims more beneficial than ours?' He replied, 'Because they spoke for the sake of aiding the religion and for the glory of Islam, while you speak for the sake of

aiding your souls and following caprice.' Or said something to that effect. Ibn 'Aṭā' Allāh ﵀ said in his *Ḥikam*: 'Every spoken word is wrapped in the garb of the heart whence it came.' This was after he had said, 'The illuminations of the wise go before their words: wherever the illumination goes, the expression reaches.' This is like the saying of the Sufis: 'What comes from the heart enters the heart, while what comes from the tongue alone goes no further than the ears.' If someone realises a spiritual state, those who enter his presence will not be unaffected by it. Understand this.

There are also three requirements for a litany's acceptance:

[1] The first is that the one who composes it be someone worthy of being followed, namely one who turns to Allah: ﴾*Follow the way of the one who turns to Me*﴿ [31:15].

[2] The second is that it be free of troublesome and ambiguous language that is outside the realm of scripture and understanding.

[3] The third is that benefit be intended from it, whether spiritual advancement or a general reminder and inspiration. Otherwise, it is nothing but tomfoolery, error or useless frivolity.

Other things that serve to perfect this are that it be free of artifice, accompanied by spiritual light [*nūr*], and issued forth from an expanded heart. The litanies of al-Shādhilī are clear examples of all of this.

The requirements for the one who uses the litany also number three, and serve to guarantee that one is truly turning to Allah:

[1] The first is that he make sure to observe the sanctity of Allah, His Messenger ﷺ and the chosen ones of His servants, while having mercy on all His creatures and giving them their rights.

[2] The second is that his deeds be valid according to the Sunna and God-consciousness. They may be further perfected by acknowledgement of Allah's blessings and a lack of any pretension,

whether outwardly or inwardly, in all movement and stillness, at all times and all situations.

[3] The third is that he govern himself with penetrating insight and sound knowledge, even if this not be by expression or eloquent speech. Then he will not be harmed if he falls into shortcomings from time to time, as long as he does not wilfully persist in them or compromise principles by deliberately directing his limbs to disobey Allah, perform insincere and artificial acts of obedience to Allah, or greedily desire the creations of Allah; for this is blindness of insight, as the Shaykh himself said (may Allah have mercy on him).

Now these conditions were met in the person of Shaykh Abū al-Ḥasan ﵁ and his litanies, so there is no good reason to deny them or say that he should not be followed. This is attested to by the stories of his spiritual states, the relations of his knowledge and the renown of his miracles, as well as how much attention was paid to him by the scholars of his time and thereafter such as ʿIzz al-Dīn ibn ʿAbd al-Salām, the Sultan of the Scholars, and the last *mujtahid* of his age. Indeed, consensus has been passed concerning the goodness of his way and the virtue of his state. Even Ibn Taymiyya spoke well of his attributes and his state; and if he refused to accept the way he approached his litanies and invocations, then this was because of his own lack of understanding; we have already indicated above how he should be rebutted. One of our shaykhs, a man of great piety, used to say that a man could swear truthfully and without any caveat that the way of the Shādhilīs is in accord with the inward state of the Companions, or words to that effect.

Allah Almighty made a man's speech a sign of his inner state, saying: ﴾*You shall know them by the tone of their speech*﴿ [47:30]. Thus a man's state may be known by three things: his speech, his character and his actions. If his speech is upright, his character illumined and his actions righteous, then he is likewise. If they are not, then he is not. The Messenger of Allah ﷺ said, *'Two qualities cannot be combined in a hypocrite: a good character and understanding of religion.'*[57] He ﷺ also said, *'Two qualities cannot be combined in a believer: stinginess and bad manners.'*[58] He ﷺ also said, *'A believer could have any quality, except treachery and deceitfulness.'*[59]

All in all, Shaykh Abū al-Ḥasan was recorded in history as one of the most distinguished men of his age and the highest ranking of all who were known; and since his time, his *ṭarīqa* has been accepted by consensus. He is one of those who may be followed, and from whom guidance may be sought, and this is because of the firmness of his religion, the perfection of his intellect, the soundness of his deeds and the firmness of his way. If any of his words are difficult to understand, then valid interpretations should be found for them just as they are for the other imams of the religion and role models of the Muslims. And if no interpretation can be found, then they should be passed over in silence; he should not be criticised merely for saying things that are ambiguous and difficult to understand as long as they are not definitely troublesome. The reason his litanies are still with us is that their blessings have been experienced and their meanings understood. Their significances are clear, and they are based on the Mighty Book; indeed, virtually every word of them is taken from it, save only for a rare few. This is clear beyond any shadow of a doubt.

Now when it comes to using these litanies, there are also three requirements which must be met:

57 Narrated by al-Tirmidhī (*Sunan, al-'Ilm*, no. 2608).
58 Narrated by al-Tirmidhī (*Sunan, al-Birr*, no. 1885).
59 Narrated by Aḥmad (*Musnad, Bāqī Musnad al-Anṣār*, no. 21149).

[1] The first is to put what has been narrated from the Prophet ﷺ first, because it is the most important and crucial thing and is the spirit that gives the litanies their vitality. This applies whether it is a case of drawing nearer to Allah and turning to Him, or of asking Him for His favour and aid, because the light and benefit of this is drawn from that, and so it is a condition for its efficacy.

[2] The second is to concentrate on their meanings as one reads them as far as one is able, because they are teachings in the guise of prayers and prayers in the guise of teachings, and knowledge accompanied by spiritual state and spiritual state aided by knowledge. This was the way of their composer (may Allah have mercy on him and be well pleased with him).

[3] The third is to avoid delving into those meanings that one does not understand without seeking an explanation, or of mentioning things of which one has no knowledge in a way that is inappropriate. Such passages should simply be read by way of quotation, and accepted for what they are. An example of this from the Litany of the Sea is the Shaykh's quotation ﴿*And lo, the hypocrites and those with sickness in their hearts say...*﴾, about which we will speak later. An example from the Great Litany [*al-Ḥizb al-Kabīr*] is his words 'For it is not of generosity...'. No one could utter such a thing except a presumptuous person or one who is quoting a presumptuous person, though it is correct in itself; and Allah knows best.

Know that the Lawgiver has given us a benefit in every desirable thing, and then the saints have then added to this. He who combines the benefit of the Law and the addition of the saints has been guided directly and also followed a spiritual guide, while he who does only one of them has missed out. However, to miss out on the direct guidance means that the benefit itself is denied, while to miss out on following a spiritual guide might not do any harm, because it only gives additional strength. To follow a spiritual guide while ignoring what has been related through the Law is harmful to both one's religion and one's worldly life. Therefore, if you wish to take on a regular *wird* from a saint, you must first act on what has been related from the Lawgiver in that regard. Let me give you seven examples to illustrate this:

[1] If you wish to use the Litany of the Sea for protection from the perils of sea travel, then you must first recite as you board, ﴾*'In the Name of Allah' be its course and its mooring; my Lord is Forgiving, Merciful*﴿ [11:41], and ﴾*They have not esteemed Allah at His true worth...*﴿ up to ﴾*Glorified and Exalted is He, above all that they associate!*﴿ [39:67], since hadiths state that this gives protection against drowning.

[2] If you wish to get out of an uncomfortable situation and find ease, then you should do what the Shaykh used to teach his companions to do, and read, 'O Vast One, O All-Knowing, O Lord of Great Bounty! You are my Lord and Your knowledge is my sufficiency. If You decree harm for me, none can remove it but You; if You wish goodness for me, none can rebuff Your grace. You give it to whom of Your servants You will, and You are the Forgiving, the Merciful.' But before this, you should invoke many prayers for forgiveness to Allah, for it has been related that Allah gives the one who does this a release from every worry and a way out of every constraint, and provides for him whence he least expects it. Use also the Prayer of Strife[60] as narrated in [*Ṣaḥīḥ*] *al-Bukhārī* and elsewhere: *'There is no god but Allah, the Clement, the Generous. There is no god but Allah, the Lord of the Mighty Throne...'* One

60 See al-Bukhārī (*Ṣaḥīḥ, al-Da'awāt*, 6346).

should also act according to the hadith narrated by Abū Dāwūd about Abū Umāma ﵁, who complained of being overwhelmed by debts and worries, so the Prophet ﷺ taught him to say: *'O Allah, I seek refuge with You from worry and grief...'* And he said, *'Say it after the dawn and sunset prayers.'*

[3] If you want help against enemies, then say what the Shaykh taught his companions to say: 'In the Name of Allah, and with Allah, and from Allah, and to Allah, and on Allah let the believers rely. O Allah, turn their plots against them, and suffice us against their evil. Allah is my Sufficiency, and that is enough. Allah hears those who call Him, and there is nothing beyond Allah. Allah is our Sufficiency, and the best of patrons.' He said that this should be said seven times after every prayer. But before this, say what the Prophet ﷺ used to say whenever he feared harm from people: *'O Allah, we seek refuge with You from their evil, and we invoke You against them.'*[61] And when he ﷺ feared an enemy he would say, *'O Allah, suffice us with whatever You will.'*[62]

[4] If you want protection from a tyrant, follow the advice of the Shaykh ﵁ by reciting Allah's words ﴿*Moses said, 'I seek refuge with my Lord and your Lord from every man who is proud and believes not in the Day of Reckoning*﴾ [40:27]. But before this, recite what the hadith recommends for those who fear a ruler or a tyrant: *'Allah is Greater; Allah is Mightier than all His creation; Allah is mightier than those I fear and those I am wary of. I seek refuge with Allah, besides whom there is no god, He who grasps heaven such that only His will keeps it from falling upon earth. [I seek refuge] from the evil of Your servant so-and-so and his forces, followers and partisans from the jinn and mankind. O Allah, be for me an ally against their*

61 Narrated with a similar wording by Abū Dāwūd (*Sunan, al-Ṣalāh*, no. 1314).
62 Narrated by al-Bayhaqī (*Dalā'il al-Nubuwwa, Ittibā' Surāqa*, no. 737).

evil. Great is Your praise, and mighty is anyone who has You as his ally. There is no god besides You.' This should be said three times, as narrated by al-Ṭabarānī and others.

[5] The Shaykh ☙ said that if you want to keep your heart from growing rusty, protect it from worry and woe and cleanse it of all sin, then say often, 'Glory be to Allah the Almighty, and praise be to Him. There is no god but Allah, and Muḥammad is the Messenger of Allah ☙. O Allah, keep knowledge of this firm in my heart, and forgive me my sins, and forgive all believing men and women.' And say, 'Praise be to Allah, and peace be upon those servants of His whom He chose.' Those who wish to read this should also read the prophetic prayer *'O Allah, I am Your servant and the child of Your servants. My forelock is in Your hand; Your decree governs me; Your judgement is fair upon me. I ask You by every Name You have, whether You have given it to Yourself, revealed it in Your Book, taught it to any of Your servants or concealed it in the unseen knowledge that is Your alone – I ask You to make the Qur'an the spring of my heart, the light of my sight, the tonic for my grief and the cure for my woes'*. The Prophet ☙ said, *'If anyone says this, Allah will dispel his woe and replace his grief with joy.'*[63]

[6] The Litany of the Sea and the protective litany that begins 'In the Name of Allah, the Protector, the Mighty...' are both meant for the purposes of seeking benefit and warding off harm. A hadith tells us that saying *'I seek refuge with the perfect Words of Allah from the evil of what He created'* three times when making camp during a journey gives safety until one sets off again.[64] *Sūrat al-Quraysh* may be recited to guard from predators, and *Sūrat al-Ikhlāṣ, al-Falaq* and *al-Nās* can be recited three times morning and evening

---

63 Narrated by Aḥmad (*Musnad, al-Mukthirīn*, no. 3528).
64 Narrated by Muslim (*Ṣaḥīḥ, al-Dhikr*, no. 4881).

to give protection from all things.[65] It is also related that saying *'In the name of Allah, against whose Name nothing can cause harm in the earth nor the sky; and He is the All-Hearing, the All-Knowing'* three times in the morning protects one from sudden tribulations until evening, and likewise saying it three times in the evening gives protection until morning.[66]

[7] The masters have recommended certain prayers and invocations for seeking wealth. A hadith teaches us to say between the two cycles of voluntary prayer before the dawn prayer and the obligatory dawn prayer, *'Glory be to Allah the Almighty, and praise be to Him. Glory be to Him who grants favours and needs no favours from others. Glory be to Him who gives protection and needs no protection from others. Glory be to Him in whose possession rests all power and might. Glory be to Him from whom glorification is a gift to those who rely on it. Glory be to Him whose praise is sung by all things. Glory be to You! There is no god but You, O You whom all things glorify! Grace me with Your pardon, for I am distressed!'* Then one should ask forgiveness of Allah one hundred times. If someone does this for forty days, all the treasures of the world will come to him willingly. Those who have tried this have found that it works.

The upshot of all this is that the efficacy of the secrets of the saints is bound by the secrets of the Sacred Law. He who wants his hopes to be realised should begin with the recommendations of the Law, and then follow them with similar things from the saints. Shaykh Abū al-ʿAbbās al-Būnī (may Allah have mercy on him) alluded to this in his book *Qabas al-Ihtidāʾ ilā Wafq al-Saʿāda* in the passage beginning, 'He who knows his litanies and invocations…', so look to it there.

65 Narrated by al-Tirmidhī (*Sunan, al-Daʿawāt,* no. 3499).
66 Narrated by Abū Dāwūd (*Sunan, al-Adab,* no. 4425).

Know also that invocation, supplication and the like cannot reverse fate or change what Allah has decreed; they are only acts of worship connected to a cause in the same way that canonical prayers are connected to their proper times, and their answers are assigned to them just as a prayer's reward is assigned to it. In sum, the answer to a supplication can come in different ways: [1] the request could be fulfilled, [2] the answer could take the form of kindness in how fate plays out, or [3] the matter could be made easy for the soul to bear so that its burning need is cooled; this is what the petitioner should really intend when he calls upon Allah, surrendering the matter to Him and thinking the best of Him in what he requests, and then following this with contentment and resignation. The Lord is the All-Knowing Opener.

INTRODUCTION – PART THREE

Why this litany is called the 'Litany of the Sea', why it was composed, how it should be used, the rulings of travel by sea and the special qualities of the sea

As for why it is called the 'Litany of the Sea', it is because it was composed at sea and for the purpose of sea travel, and the first time it was used was at sea, and because of the seas that are mentioned and described therein. It is also because it is itself a sea of knowledge and potency, such that anyone who attempted to explain it as it really is would not be able to exhaust its meanings. This can be illustrated by considering only the *fawātiḥ* in it, meaning the symbolic Arabic letters from the beginnings of certain chapters of the Qur'an. ʿAlī (may Allah ennoble his face) said that if he willed, he could have filled seventy camel-loads of pages on the meaning of *Kāf Ha Yā ʿAyn Ṣād*. The same can be said about the other letters.

As for why it was composed, the Shaykh travelled on the Red Sea on his way to the pilgrimage, along with a Christian man. They were delayed for a few days because of poor winds. During this time, he saw the Prophet ﷺ in a dream, who gave him glad tidings and taught the Litany to him. He read it, and then told the Christian man to ready the ship for sail. He said, 'But where is the wind?' The Shaykh said, 'Do it, for the wind is coming even as we speak.' It proved to be as he said, and the Christian entered Islam. I have told this story before, so look to it there.

As for how to use the Litany, it differs according to intention and spiritual aspiration. It is used for the purpose of bringing benefit and warding off harm, and the specific intention should be made at the words *and subject to us this sea*. This is what Ibn 'Abbād (may Allah have mercy on him) said, as I have seen in his own handwriting, and it is correct. Ibn 'Āṭā' Allāh said in *Laṭā'if al-Minan*, 'It is a *wird* for after the afternoon ['*aṣr*] prayer, while the Great Litany is for after the dawn prayer.' I might add to this that the *Munājāt* [concluding prayers] of the *Ḥikam* of Ibn 'Aṭā' Allāh should be read in the final part of the night before dawn. Each of them has its own secret, as the one who sticks to them will discover in no short time if he holds to piety and righteousness without taking on too much; and Allah knows best.

As for the ruling about travelling by sea in itself, there is no difference of opinion today that it is permitted, although some of the early Muslims did differ on the matter. It is prohibited in five circumstances:

[1] If it necessitates leaving the obligatory prayers or performing them incorrectly. Mālik was asked about boarding a ship that is rocking so violently that one cannot pray, and said, 'Woe unto him who leaves the prayer!'

[2] If the sea is so rough there is a reasonable fear of drowning. In such a situation it is not permitted to board because this would amount to suicide. They say that this is from when the sun enters Scorpio until the end of winter.

[3] If it is feared that the passengers may be captured and that the enemy may kill people and seize property, then it is not permitted to board, unless there are guards on board and the Muslims are strong enough to resist such attacks.

[4] If boarding them puts one in a situation where one is subservient to the non-Muslims' rules and under their power, and forced to witness their evil conduct, even if one's life and possessions are safe because one has a treaty with them. This is the condition of the Muslims nowadays when they board ships alongside people who engage in gambling and the like. Some scholars have said that this is equivalent to engaging in trade in enemy lands; the well-known position of the [Mālikī] school is that this is reprehensible [*makrūh*], which technically means it is lawful. This is why some great scholars and righteous men have boarded ships in such conditions; it seems they felt the reprehensible status of the action was excusable when it was done in order to fulfil an obligation such as the pilgrimage and the like. Now when Shaykh Abū al-Ḥasan رضي الله عنه boarded the ship with the Christian man, this was not one of those kinds of journeys, because the sea was under Muslim rule and the Christian was not an enemy, and allowed him to board the ship because he feared him or had made an agreement with him; he was not his captain, but his employee. Mālik deemed it permissible to hire a Christian camel-driver if he has the best manners and character of all the available candidates. Ibn Farḥūn said, 'Hiring a Muslim who does not pray would be less troublesome than this, so there is even more reason for such to be permitted,' but this is questionable reasoning.

[5] If it is feared that one will not be able to cover oneself properly, such as if a woman boards a small vessel where she has nowhere

to conceal herself. Mālik deemed this forbidden even in the case of the pilgrimage, only allowing it if she is given a private place in a large vessel, according to the well-known opinion.

As for the special qualities of the sea, it would take too long to mention them all and we could not fulfil such a task. It is enough to say that it is all mercy and blessing on the one hand, and survival and peril on the other. Its surface is a road for ships to pass over; its interior is full of precious pearls; its waves are perilous; its water is purifying; its carrion is lawful. Al-Dāraquṭnī narrated that the angels use its water for purification when they ascend and descend. 'Umar ibn al-Khaṭṭāb ؓ said to 'Amr ibn al-'Āṣ ؓ, 'Describe the sea for me.' He said, 'O Commander of the Faithful, it is a mighty creation. Tiny and weak creatures sail upon it, like maggots on a plank of wood.' 'Umar said, 'Indeed, were it not for the pilgrimage and jihad, I would beat all who travel upon it with a whip!' Then he forbade travel on it, and then relented and allowed it again after a time. The same thing happened during the rules of 'Uthmān ﵁ and Muʿāwiya ﵁, until finally a consensus was reached that it is lawful as long as its conditions are met; and all grace is from Allah.

It is now time to set about the task at hand, namely to explain the words of the Litany in a way that is easy and understandable. Allah alone opens the way to success and ease, and He is our Sufficiency and the best of patrons.

In the name of Allah, the Compassionate, the Merciful
Praise be to Allah, Lord of the Worlds. May blessings and peace be upon our master Muḥammad, noblest of prophets and messengers, and upon his Family and Companions.

THE *ḤIZB AL-BAḤR* OF IMAM SHĀDHILĪ رضي الله عنه

O Allah, O High, O Great, O Clement, O All-Knowing; You are my Lord and Your knowledge is my sufficiency; how perfect, then, is my Lord, how perfect my sufficiency! You give victory to whom You will, and You are the Almighty, the Merciful.

We ask Your protection, in movements and rests, in words and desires and thoughts; from the doubts, suppositions, and fancies that veil hearts from beholding things unseen. For ﴾the believers have been tried, and mightily shaken; and lo, the hypocrites and those with sickness in their hearts say: Allah and His Messenger have promised us nothing but delusion﴿ [33:11–12].

So make us steadfast, give us victory, and subject to us this sea, as You subjected the sea to Moses, the fire to Abraham, the mountains and iron to David, the wind and demons and jinn to

بِسْمِ اللهِ الرَّحْمَـٰنِ الرَّحِيمِ

الْحَمْدُ لِلهِ رَبِّ الْعَالَمِينَ، وَالصَّلَاةُ وَالسَّلَامُ عَلَى سَيِّدِنَا مُحَمَّدٍ أَشْرَفِ الْأَنْبِيَاءِ وَالْمُرْسَلِينَ وَعَلَى آلِهِ وَصَحْبِهِ وَسَلَّمَ .

حِزْبُ الْبَحْرِ

لِلْإِمَامِ الشَّاذِلِي رَضِيَ اللَّهُ عَنْهُ

اَللَّهُمَّ يَا عَلِيُّ، يَا عَظِيمُ، يَا حَلِيمُ، يَا عَلِيمُ، أَنْتَ رَبِّي وَعِلْمُكَ حَسْبِي، فَنِعْمَ الرَّبُّ رَبِّي وَنِعْمَ الْحَسْبُ حَسْبِي، تَنْصُرُ مَنْ تَشَاءُ وَأَنْتَ الْعَزِيزُ الرَّحِيمُ،

نَسْأَلُكَ الْعِصْمَةَ فِي الْحَرَكَاتِ وَالسَّكَنَاتِ وَالْكَلِمَاتِ وَالْإِرَادَاتِ وَالْخَطَرَاتِ مِنَ الشُّكُوكِ وَالظُّنُونِ وَالْأَوْهَامِ السَّاتِرَةِ لِلْقُلُوبِ عَنْ مُطَالَعَةِ الْغُيُوبِ، فَقَدْ ﴿ٱبْتُلِيَ الْمُؤْمِنُونَ وَزُلْزِلُوا زِلْزَالاً شَدِيداً﴾، ﴿وَإِذْ يَقُولُ الْمُنَافِقُونَ وَالَّذِينَ فِي قُلُوبِهِمْ مَرَضٌ مَّا وَعَدَنَا اللهُ وَرَسُولُهُ إِلَّا غُرُوراً﴾،

فَثَبِّتْنَا وَانْصُرْنَا، وَسَخِّرْ لَنَا هَذَا الْبَحْرَ كَمَا سَخَّرْتَ الْبَحْرَ لِمُوسَى عَلَيْهِ السَّلَامُ، وَسَخَّرْتَ النَّارَ لِإِبْرَاهِيمَ عَلَيْهِ السَّلَامُ، وَسَخَّرْتَ الْجِبَالَ

Solomon. Subject to us every sea You possess, in the earth and the sky, the kingdom and the dominion, the sea of this life and the sea of the life to come. Subject to us everything, O You in whose hand is dominion of everything!

﴾*Kāf Ha Yā ʿAyn Ṣād*﴿ [19:1] (3)

Give us victory, for You are the best who give victory.

Clear our vision, for You are the best who clear visions.

Forgive us, for You are the best of forgivers.

Have mercy on us, for You are the best of the merciful.

Give us sustenance, for You are the best of providers.

Guide us, and save us from the wrongdoing folk.

Give us a goodly wind, as may be in Your knowledge; loose it upon us from the storehouses of Your mercy; and carry us upon it in honour, with safety and wellbeing in our religion, in our life in this world, and in the world to come. Truly, You have power over all things.

O Allah, give us ease in our affairs, with peace for our hearts and bodies, and safety and wellbeing in our worldly life and our religion.

Be our companion in our travels, and keep watch over our families in our stead.

Blot out the faces of our enemies, and fix them where they stand, so they can neither move nor reach us.

وَالْحَدِيدَ لِدَاوُدَ عَلَيْهِ السَّلَامُ، وَسَخَّرْتَ الرِّيحَ وَالشَّيَاطِينَ وَالْجِنَّ
لِسُلَيْمَانَ عَلَيْهِ السَّلَامُ، وَسَخِّرْ لَنَا كُلَّ بَحْرٍ هُوَ لَكَ فِي الْأَرْضِ
وَالسَّمَآءِ، وَالْمُلْكِ وَالْمَلَكُوتِ، وَبَحْرَ الدُّنْيَا وَبَحْرَ الْآخِرَةِ، وَسَخِّرْ
لَنَا كُلَّ شَيْءٍ، يَا مَنْ بِيَدِهِ مَلَكُوتُ كُلِّ شَيْءٍ،
كٓهيعٓصٓ، كٓهيعٓصٓ، كٓهيعٓصٓ،

اُنْصُرْنَا فَإِنَّكَ خَيْرُ النَّاصِرِينَ، وَافْتَحْ لَنَا فَإِنَّكَ خَيْرُ الْفَاتِحِينَ،
وَاغْفِرْ لَنَا فَإِنَّكَ خَيْرُ الْغَافِرِينَ، وَارْحَمْنَا فَإِنَّكَ خَيْرُ الرَّاحِمِينَ،
وَارْزُقْنَا فَإِنَّكَ خَيْرُ الرَّازِقِينَ، وَاهْدِنَا وَنَجِّنَا مِنَ الْقَوْمِ
الظَّالِمِينَ،وَهَبْ لَنَا رِيحاً طَيِّبَةً كَمَا هِيَ فِي عِلْمِكَ، وَانْشُرْهَا عَلَيْنَا
مِنْ خَزَائِنِ رَحْمَتِكَ، وَاحْمِلْنَا بِهَا حَمْلَ الْكَرَامَةِ مَعَ السَّلَامَةِ
وَالْعَافِيَةِ فِي الدِّينِ وَالدُّنْيَا وَالْآخِرَةِ إِنَّكَ عَلَى كُلِّ شَيْءٍ قَدِيرٌ،

اَللَّهُمَّ يَسِّرْ لَنَا أُمُورَنَا مَعَ الرَّاحَةِ لِقُلُوبِنَا وَأَبْدَانِنَا، مَعَ السَّلَامَةِ
وَالْعَافِيَةِ فِي دِينِنَا وَدُنْيَانَا،
وَكُنْ لَنَا صَاحِباً فِي سَفَرِنَا، وَخَلِيفَةً فِي أَهْلِنَا،

وَاطْمِسْ عَلَى وُجُوهِ أَعْدَائِنَا، وَامْسَخْهُمْ عَلَى مَكَانَتِهِمْ فَلَا
يَسْتَطِيعُونَ الْمُضِيَّ وَلَا الْمَجِيءَ إِلَيْنَا،

﴾Had We willed, We would have blotted out their eyes; and they would race to the path, but how should they see? Or had We willed, We would have fixed them where they stood, so they neither could go forward, nor return﴿ [36:66–67].

﴾*Yā Sīn*. By the Wise Qur'an, truly you are of the messengers, upon a straight path. This is a revelation of the Almighty, the Merciful; that you might warn a people whose forefathers were not warned, so they heed not. Already has sentence been passed against most of them, so they believe not. Verily, We have placed shackles on their necks, even up to the chins, so they bend not. And We have placed a barrier before them, and a barrier behind them, and enshrouded them, so that they see not﴿ [36:1–9].

Disfigured be those faces! (3)
﴾And faces shall be humbled before the Eternal Living, the All-Sustaining; while whoever bears wrongdoing shall have failed﴿ [20:111].

Ṭā Sīn. Ḥā Mīm, 'Ayn Sīn Qāf.
﴾He has loosed the two seas; they come together, but between them is a barrier they do not cross﴿ [55:19–20].

Ḥā Mīm (7)
The matter is done, the victory come. Against us they shall not be helped.

﴿وَلَوْ نَشَاءُ لَطَمَسْنَا عَلَى أَعْيُنِهِمْ فَاسْتَبَقُوا الصِّرَاطَ فَأَنَّى يُبْصِرُونَ، وَلَوْ نَشَاءُ لَمَسَخْنَاهُمْ عَلَى مَكَانَتِهِمْ فَمَا اسْتَطَاعُوا مُضِيًّا وَلَا يَرْجِعُونَ﴾،

﴿يس، وَالْقُرْآنِ الْحَكِيمِ، إِنَّكَ لَمِنَ الْمُرْسَلِينَ، عَلَى صِرَاطٍ مُسْتَقِيمٍ، تَنْزِيلَ الْعَزِيزِ الرَّحِيمِ، لِتُنْذِرَ قَوْمًا مَا أُنْذِرَ آبَاؤُهُمْ فَهُمْ غَافِلُونَ، لَقَدْ حَقَّ الْقَوْلُ عَلَى أَكْثَرِهِمْ فَهُمْ لَا يُؤْمِنُونَ، إِنَّا جَعَلْنَا فِي أَعْنَاقِهِمْ أَغْلَالًا فَهِيَ إِلَى الْأَذْقَانِ فَهُمْ مُقْمَحُونَ، وَجَعَلْنَا مِنْ بَيْنِ أَيْدِيهِمْ سَدًّا وَمِنْ خَلْفِهِمْ سَدًّا فَأَغْشَيْنَاهُمْ فَهُمْ لَا يُبْصِرُونَ﴾،

شَاهَتِ الْوُجُوهُ، شَاهَتِ الْوُجُوهُ، شَاهَتِ الْوُجُوهُ،

﴿وَعَنَتِ الْوُجُوهُ لِلْحَيِّ الْقَيُّومِ، وَقَدْ خَابَ مَنْ حَمَلَ ظُلْمًا﴾،

طس، حم عسق،

﴿مَرَجَ الْبَحْرَيْنِ يَلْتَقِيَانِ بَيْنَهُمَا بَرْزَخٌ لَا يَبْغِيَانِ﴾،

(حم، حم، حم، حم، حم، حم، حم،)
حُمَّ الْأَمْرُ، وَجَاءَ النَّصْرُ، فَعَلَيْنَا لَا يُنْصَرُونَ

﴾*Ḥā Mīm*. The revelation of the Book from Allah, the Almighty, the All-Knowing: Forgiver of Sins, Accepter of Repentance, Terrible in Punishment, Infinite in Bounty: no god is there but He; unto Him is the final becoming﴿ [40:1–3].

Bismi'Llāh is our door,

Tabāraka our walls,

Yā Sīn our roof,

Kāf Hā Yā 'Ayn Ṣād our sufficiency,

Ḥā Mīm, 'Ayn Sīn Qāf our protection.

﴾Allah will suffice you against them, and He is the All-Hearing, the All-Knowing﴿ [2:137]. (3)

The veil of the Throne has been dropped over us; the eye of Allah is gazing upon us; by the power of Allah none shall overcome us; ﴾And Allah encompasses them from behind: Nay, it is a noble recitation, in a guarded tablet﴿ [85:20–22].

﴾For Allah is best as protector, and He is the Most Merciful of the merciful﴿ [12:64]. (3)

﴾Verily, Allah is my Patron, He who revealed down the Book; and He looks after the righteous﴿ [7:196]. (3)

﴾Allah is my Sufficiency, there is no god but He; on Him I rely, and He is Lord of the Mighty Throne﴿ [9:129]. (3)

In the name of Allah, against whose Name nothing can cause

﴿حمٓ، تَنزِيلُ الْكِتَابِ مِنَ اللهِ الْعَزِيزِ الْعَلِيمِ، غَافِرِ الذَّنْبِ وَقَابِلِ التَّوْبِ، شَدِيدِ الْعِقَابِ، ذِي الطَّوْلِ، لَآ إِلَٰهَ إِلَّا هُوَ إِلَيْهِ الْمَصِيرُ﴾،

بِسْمِ اللهِ بَابُنَا،

تَبَارَكَ حِيطَانُنَا،

يسٓ سَقْفُنَا،

كٓهيعٓصٓ كِفَايَتُنَا،

حمٓ عٓسٓقٓ حِمَايَتُنَا

﴿فَسَيَكْفِيكَهُمُ اللهُ وَهُوَ السَّمِيعُ الْعَلِيمُ - ثلاثا﴾،

سِتْرُ الْعَرْشِ مَسْبُولٌ عَلَيْنَا، وَعَيْنُ اللهِ نَاظِرَةٌ إِلَيْنَا، بِحَوْلِ اللهِ لَا يُقْدَرُ عَلَيْنَا، ﴿وَاللهُ مِن وَرَآئِهِم مُّحِيطٌ، بَلْ هُوَ قُرْءَانٌ مَّجِيدٌ فِي لَوْحٍ مَّحْفُوظٍ﴾،

﴿ فَاللهُ خَيْرٌ حَافِظاً وَهُوَ أَرْحَمُ الرَّاحِمِينَ - ثلاثا - ﴾،

﴿ إِنَّ وَلِيِّيَ اللهُ الَّذِي نَزَّلَ الْكِتَابَ وَهُوَ يَتَوَلَّى الصَّالِحِينَ - ثلاثا - ﴾، (فَإِن تَوَلَّوْا فَقُلْ حَسْبِيَ اللهُ لَآ إِلَٰهَ إِلَّا هُوَ عَلَيْهِ تَوَكَّلْتُ وَهُوَ رَبُّ الْعَرْشِ الْعَظِيمِ، - ثلاثا-﴾،

(بِسْمِ اللهِ الَّذِي لَا يَضُرُّ مَعَ اسْمِهِ شَيْءٌ فِي الْأَرْضِ وَلَا فِي

harm in the earth nor the sky; and He is the All-Hearing, the All-Knowing. (3)

There is no power, and no strength, save by Allah, the High, the Great.

and may Allah bless our master Muhammad and his family and his companions and grant them much peace, and praise belongs to Allah the Lord of the worlds. Help from Allah and a near opening. And give good news to the believers. He is the First and the Last and the Outwardly Manifest and the Inwardly Hidden and He has knowledge of every thing. Nothing is like Him and He is the All-Hearing the All-Seeing. Blessed as a Master and blessed as a Helpr Your forgiveness O our Lord and to You is the homecoming.,

السَّمَآءِ وَهُوَ السَّمِيعُ الْعَلِيمُ - ثلاثا -)،
(وَلَا حَوْلَ وَلَا قُوَّةَ إِلَّا بِاللهِ الْعَلِيّ الْعَظِيمِ - ثلاثا -)،

وَصَلَّى اللهُ عَلَى سَيِّدِنَا مُحَمَّدٍ وَعَلَىٓ آلِهِ وَصَحْبِهِ وَسَلَّمَ تَسْلِيماً كَثِيراً، وَالْحَمْدُ لِلهِ رَبِّ الْعَالَمِينَ، نَصْرٌ مِّنَ اللهِ وَفَتْحٌ قَرِيبٌ، وَبَشِّرِ الْمُؤْمِنِينَ، هُوَ الْأَوَّلُ وَالْآخِرُ وَالظَّاهِرُ وَالْبَاطِنُ، وَهُوَ بِكُلِّ شَيْءٍ عَلِيمٌ، لَيْسَ كَمِثْلِهِ شَيْءٌ وَهُوَ السَّمِيعُ الْبَصِيرُ نِعْمَ الْمَوْلَى وَنِعْمَ النَّصِيرُ، غُفْرَانَكَ رَبَّنَا وَإِلَيْكَ الْمَصِيرُ .

Commentary

O Allah, O High, O Great, O Clement, O All-Knowing; You are my Lord and Your knowledge is my sufficiency; how perfect, then, is my Lord, how perfect my sufficiency! You give victory to whom You will, and You are the Almighty, the Merciful.

The Shaykh begins the Litany with these words because they evoke the might of lordship and the humility of servitude, and how one should find sufficiency in His knowledge, and return to Him at all times, and surrender one's affair to Him whether the outcome is desirable or not, praising Him all the while and lauding the perfection of His Essence first, and His Act last. To turn to Him completely is to be conscious of all this; for if one turns to Him without being conscious of the might of His lordship and the humility of one's servitude, this is nothing but a show. This explains why many people do not benefit from reciting personal prayers and invocations that truly bear the promise of an answer, and are answered for those who recite them with sincerity and devotion.

To find sufficiency in His knowledge, while thinking the best of Him and leaving it up to Him to decide whether to answer the prayer, is part of the etiquette of praying, and a pillar of its efficacy. Shaykh Muḥammad 'Abd al-'Azīz al-Mahdawī ☙ even said, 'If a person does not abandon his own will when he prays, content with whatever the Real wills for him, he is merely the object of a divine ruse, and is one of those about whom Allah says [to the angels], *"Meet his need, for I hate to hear his voice."*[67] If one is content with the will of the Real, and not his own will, then his prayer is answered, even if he is not given what he seeks; for what matters is the ultimate consequence of a deed.'

Now in these opening words, ten divine Names are mentioned: seven plainly, and three more by allusion; that is, they are understood implicitly, if not stated explicitly as the other seven are.

The seven explicit Names are: the High, the Great, the Clement, the All-Knowing, the Lord, the Almighty and the Merciful. As for the three implicit Names, they are: the Sufficient, the Giver of Victory and the Doer of What He Will. Concerning the meanings of these Names:

The High is He upon whose mention and description all else becomes small. *The Great* is He with whom nothing shares any common measure in His exaltedness and majesty, whether in essence, quality, name or deed. Now He is High in His greatness, above the greatness of any other; and He is Great in His highness, beyond any conception of highness that does not befit His Essence. Thus the two Names are interrelated, the meaning of each of them pertinent to the other, such that the attribute is raised to the furthest limit of its meaning.

The Clement is He who is not driven by wrath to hasten the retribution incurred by those who disobey Him; He gives the sinner time, though He does not neglect him. If He forgoes the

---

67 Part of a Sacred Hadith narrated by al-Ṭabarānī (*Awsaṭ, Bāb al-Mīm*, 8678).

punishment all together, He is Forgiving and Merciful.

The All-Knowing is He whose knowledge encompasses all things, whether they exist outwardly or not, without any exceptions or conditions. He knows the sins of His servants, yet does not hasten their punishment out of clemency. This is an aspect of His greatness and exaltedness, which were manifested in the sea and allowed us to travel upon it.

The divine Names mentioned here are apt, then, because the sea is a creation endowed with greatness and exalted status, and in it are manifested Allah's greatness and loftiness, inasmuch as He subdued it for mankind and bent it to their will, so that they could eat fresh meat from it, adorn themselves with ornaments from it, and sail upon it by His will. Thus the high status and greatness of the sea only point to the greatness and exaltedness of Him who subdued it.

Furthermore, the sea is traversed by the righteous and the sinner alike, and in His mercy and kindness He does not unleash it open them, though He knows well the sins they commit. Indeed, if you consider the matter you will see that those who work at sea and are always returning to it are the most sinful and rebellious of people. This shows how travel upon the sea is a pure grace and mercy of Allah, and material means have nothing to do with it.

The sea is thus a sign of the greatness of Allah in His Essence and His Qualities, and of His knowledge of what mankind does upon it; and all this is an aspect of His greatness in Essence, Qualities and Acts, for there is nothing greater than clemency accompanied by knowledge, and nothing stronger than greatness accompanied by exaltedness.

It has been said that these opening words contain the Supreme Name of Allah, and Ibn ʿAbd al-Barr deemed this to be the strongest view. It is the origin of the root, and the place to which all the branches lead back. Someone heard in his sleep: 'Every Name whose meaning is found in all the other Names can be called the Supreme Name; of the Most Beautiful Names, there are seven of these, one of which is *the Great*, though *the Compassionate* is not one of them.' Now this is suggested by the hadiths on the subject, for it could be said of every hadith that speaks of the Supreme Name, despite the different wordings and various Names and Qualities therein, which are variously given as single names, compound names, and phrases. Understand this.

So the meaning of His Names *the High* and *the Great* flow through other Names such as *the All-Knowing* and *the Clement*, because He is High in His clemency and knowledge, and Great in all of them. Because of how the meanings of these two Names flow through all meanings that could be attached to the Essence, the Qualities and the Acts, they occur at the climax of the *Āyat al-Kursī*, which begins with the Names of the Essence, then describes the Qualities, then describes the Acts and their objects. Understand this.

Now whosoever knows that He is the High and the Great will find his heart filled with magnification and reverence, and his spirit will be marked by them, and his innermost secret heart will be expanded with them. He will pay no more heed to his own ego, nor be content with anything but Allah. And whosoever knows that Allah is the All-Knowing and the Clement, and thus hopes for His kindness and thinks the best of Him at all times, will no longer have any regard for the sea or for anything else, for he will be occupied by his Lord and annihilated in Him and in nothing else. He will say, with every atom of his being:

You are my Lord, and there is no other lord;

How could I have any lord but You?

That is, 'Because of the perfection of His greatness and exaltedness, I care for nothing but Him, and turn to no one but Him, and hope for no benefit nor fear any harm from anyone but Him.'

The Lord is the Sovereign, who takes care of His servants with kindness. There is no king but He, and no director but He. The Shaykh's words *You are my Lord* are a disavowal of attachment to anything besides Him.

The Shaykh's words *Your knowledge is my sufficiency* express sufficiency in the knowledge of Allah; this in turn means to surrender one's state entirely to Allah, and to look to what He has without relying on one's own soul.

The meaning of *my sufficiency* is that it is enough for me in the state that I am in; this evokes the Friend of Allah, Abraham عليه السلام, when he was cast into the pit of fire and Gabriel came to him and said, 'Have you any need?' He replied, 'Not of you, but of my Lord.' Gabriel said, 'Then ask Him.' Abraham replied: 'I need not ask, for it suffices me that He knows my state.'

This is the way of the gnostics when all means have been exhausted: to seek refuge in the divine knowledge by surrendering to it and not even asking. It is different when some means are still at hand, for in that case they must be utilised. Consider how Moses's عليه السلام mother was commanded to cast him into the water, and how the angels answered Lot عليه السلام by saying ﴾*Your Lord's decree is surely at hand*﴿ [11:76] after he had said to his people ﴾*Had I only power over you, or recourse to a strong pillar!*﴿ [77:80]. He عليه السلام wanted to utilise some kind of means against them, if he had it, and the answer he was given was that the decree had come to pass, and that it was not the time for material means. The Prophet

ﷺ alluded to this when he said, *'May Allah have mercy on Lot! He sought recourse in a strong pillar.'*[68] He felt compassion for him because of how he thought that means were still available to him; those who have no share of inner realities will not understand this, and this will lead them to error. Understand this.

Know that there are three forms of turning to Allah at times of need:

The first is to turn to Him in absolute surrender. This is what one does when all the means have been exhausted, as has just been described.

The second is to turn to Him with requests and petitions. This is what one does at times of the heart's expansion during normal circumstances, to remind the soul of its need for Allah when it has become oblivious to His Oneness and to our dire need for Him. It may also be employed as a means of teaching, reminding or the like.

The third is to turn to Him by consigning the affair to Him entirely. This is what one does when one thinks the best of Him and suffices oneself with His knowledge and with the truth of His Oneness, and busies oneself with His remembrance. This evokes the words of Abraham عليه السلام ﴾*And He it is whom I hope will forgive my sins on Judgement Day*﴿ [26:82], the words of Moses عليه السلام ﴾*Lord, for any good that You might send down to me, I am in dire need!*﴿ [28:24] and the words of our Prophet ﷺ *'I am not without need of Your clemency; Your clemency more than suffices me!'*, and so on. They have said:

Should I mention my need, or does Your shyness suffice me?
For indeed, among Your Qualities is shyness:

68 Narrated by al-Bukhārī (*Ṣaḥīḥ, Aḥādīth al-Anbiyā',* 3121) and Muslim (*Ṣaḥīḥ, al-Īmān,* 216).

If a man sings Your praises one day,
>His praise spares him the need to display himself.

Now since the sea cannot be subdued by material means, the way to approach it is to consign the matter entirely to Allah; yet since the business of voyaging upon the sea involves the employment of material means, it is also apt to ask His help therein. Therefore the Shaykh combines them both, as you can see.

The Shaykh's words *how perfect, then, is my Lord, how perfect my sufficiency* evoke a sense of great praise, so that the soul is more content with Him than with whatever it wishes to ask of Him, through consciousness of the grandeur of the setting. Otherwise, these words express a perfect truth, for of course He is the most perfect of masters and the most perfect of helpers. Given this, anyone who attaches himself to Him will not be disappointed, nor will anyone who trusts Him be neglected, as He says: ❲*Whoso trusts in Allah, He is his sufficiency*❳ [65:3]; that is, his provider, redeemer and helper.

Allah told us of certain people, saying: ❲*Those unto whom men said: 'Lo, the people have gathered against you, therefore fear them!' Yet this only increased them in faith, and they said: 'Allah is sufficient for us, and supremely to be trusted is He!'; and they returned with grace and favour from Allah, and no evil touched them, and they sought after the good pleasure of Allah...*❳ [3:173–174]. Thus He declared that those who speak this invocation[69] with sincerity will receive grace and favour, and be guarded from evil, and will attain unto divinely granted success; and He then offered them even more besides it, saying: ❲*...And Allah is of Infinite Bounty*❳

---

69 'Allah is sufficient for us, and supremely to be trusted is He!' (*Ḥasbunā 'Llāhu wa ni'ma 'l-wakīl.*)

[3:174].

Imam Mālik's ❀ ring was engraved with *Allah is sufficient for us, and supremely to be trusted is He!*, and someone asked him why this was. He replied, 'It reminds me of this truth.' Understand this.

The Shaykh's words *You give victory to whom You will, and You are the Almighty, the Merciful* are on the level of deference to the divine will: Allah does what He will, and His verdict cannot be challenged, and nothing happens but what He wills to happen; for He is the Almighty, who overcomes and cannot be overcome, and the All-Powerful, whose command cannot be rebuffed, so that all one can do is submit to Him. He is the Merciful, who has mercy on His servants by providing them with such supports as help towards victory. Thus His might is manifested in those against whom the victory is given, and His mercy is manifested in those to whom the victory is given; He shows mercy to the latter with the very same thing that deals defeat to the former. The Almighty says: ❮*He punishes whom He will, and shows mercy to whom He will; and unto Him you will be turned*❯ [29:21].

In sum, with these opening words the Shaykh summarises the divine Oneness, faith and inner truth, all in the light of the grandeur of lordship and the neediness of servitude. He opened the Great Litany in the same way, beginning it with the words of Allah ❮*When they who believe in Our signs come to you...*❯ [6:54], evoking the rays of mercy in the heart of majesty, and the breadth of majesty in the heart of mercy.

※

We ask Your protection, in movements and rests, in words and desires and thoughts; from the doubts, suppositions and fancies that veil hearts from beholding things unseen. For the believers have been tried, and mightily shaken; and lo, the hypocrites and those with sickness in their hearts say: 'Allah and His Messenger have promised us nothing but delusion.'

The Shaykh then asks his Lord for infallible protection [*ʿiṣma*], which means prevention of sin by the divine Will in a way that cannot be violated because it has been ordained by Allah, although the act of sin is itself intrinsically possible. What is being asked for here is protection from those things which veil one from Allah in any way, because the veil is the root of every trial, just as protection from it is the root of all safety. It has even been said that it means to be prevented from sin such that it is impossible that one could fall into it, that is, a complete prevention of it – by the ordain of Allah ﷻ, not because it is intrinsically impossible.

Now this protection is granted to those whom Allah elects, whether prophets, saints or others, but it is necessary in the case of the prophets and must not be questioned for them, whilst it should not be claimed for any non-prophet, since it is possible for all but the prophets to sin. Non-prophets may be said to have been given protection [*ḥifẓ*] from sin whilst still technically being able to fall into it. Outwardly speaking, the prophets are infallible [*maʿṣūm*], while the saints are protected [*maḥfūẓ*]. Yet an occurrence of *ḥifẓ* might well be *ʿiṣma* in Allah's knowledge, although we have no way of acquiring it, even though we may ask for it and it is intrinsically possible. Allah knows best, and He has said: ﴾*Whoso seeks protection* [*yaʿtaṣim*] *from Allah has been guided to a straight path*﴿ [3:101], and Noah ﷺ said: ﴾*There is no protector* [*ʿāṣim*] *from Allah's command, save for those on whom He has mercy*﴿ [11:43].

So the Shaykh's ﵁ words *We ask Your protection* mean: We ask You to guard us from sins by concealing them so we do not know how to get to them, and so they do not enter our thoughts or occur to us at any time. We ask for protection *in movements*, namely motions left and right, and to and fro; and in *rests*, namely times when we are motionless and fixed in one place. He says *movements* in the plural because of how diverse they are.

We ask for protection *in words*, namely the movements of the tongue and the heart which form words and statements; in *desires*, namely the decisive movement of the heart which produce inclinations towards deeds and words; and in *thoughts*, namely the movements of the interior voices which produce actions, the first of these being whim, which is not necessarily acted upon, and the last of them being firm resolve, which is always acted upon; there are various opinions about the stages between them.

Now these five[70] are the channels for good and bad deeds, and the things concerning them from which one should seek protection are *the doubts, suppositions and fancies that veil hearts from beholding things unseen*: the unseen secrets of gnosis, of lordship, and of faith; he who is veiled from them is caught in woes and worries, to which Sidi Ibn ʿAṭāʾ Allāh alluded in his *Ḥikam* when he said: 'If hearts experience worry and sadness, it is because they are lacking in vision.'

His words *that veil...* describe *suppositions, doubts and fancies*, which sometimes veil and sometimes do not; he seeks refuge from the former because of the obstacle they constitute, and leaves aside the latter because they may be in agreement with the truth, or at least not opposed to it.[71]

70 Movement, rest, speech, desire and thought.

71 That is, it is possible to suppose or imagine something that is actually true.

With these words, the Shaykh ﷺ lists all the psychological motions and defects, thereby providing a definition for the soul and its defects, just as in the previous sentence he spoke of the Almighty Lord and His perfection. This is the epitome of beneficial knowledge and consummate truth. Junayd ﷺ was asked about beneficial knowledge, and replied: 'It is to know your Lord, and not to oppose your destiny.' This is what lies at the heart of the Shaykh's words here, so do your best to contemplate them; and all success is from Allah.

Now concerning *suppositions, doubts and fancies*, 'supposition' means that which is more likely to be true than false; 'doubt' means that which is equally likely to be true or false; and 'fancy' means that which is likely untrue. In each case, the thing in question might either be good, or evil. The Shaykh here asks that they all be done away with before they become firm, lest it become impossible to get rid of them thereafter. It is said, 'Guard yourself against the ruin of misgivings, before worries overcome you and damage you.' It is also said, 'Sin starts with a thought, just as rain starts with a drop.' The Messenger of Allah ﷺ himself said: *'Beware of supposition, for supposition is the falsest of speech.'*[72]

Foul suppositions always come from foul hearts, and are neither on the side of the Real nor the side of man. Someone said:

When a man's deeds are evil, his suppositions are evil,
And he comes to believe his own deluded fancies;
He attacks his lovers with the words of his enemy,
And enters into a dark night of doubt.

72 Narrated by al-Bukhārī (*Ṣaḥīḥ, al-Nikāḥ*, 4747) and Muslim (*Ṣaḥīḥ, al-Birr wal-Ṣila wal-Adab*, 4646).

It is related that the Messenger of Allah ﷺ said: *'Two traits beyond which there is nothing more evil: to think ill of Allah, and to think ill of His servants. And two traits beyond which there is nothing better: to think well of Allah, and to think well of His servants.'*

Shaykh Abū al-Ḥasan ؓ himself said:

> One night, I recited *Sūrat al-Nās*, and a voice said to me: 'The most evil of whispering is that which comes between you and one you love, reminding you of his sins and causing you to forget his good deeds, and exaggerating your pessimism and diminishing your optimism, thus pulling you away from thinking well of Allah and His Messenger ﷺ and towards thinking ill of Allah. Beware this trap, for it has ensnared many servants, ascetics, and men of piety and righteousness.'

Perfect wellbeing is for the heart to find peace in Allah by means of the certitude that leads to contentment and resignation. All trial comes from doubt, hesitation and flitting to and fro among swarms of thoughts that never let one live in peace and stability. These suppositions, doubts and fancies are manifested in open trials and tribulations; Allah sends them to His believing servants to separate the wheat from the chaff. They cause those who have faith to increase in faith, and those who are hypocrites to manifest their unbelief and wickedness.

All this means that the believers should turn back to Allah in hope, seeking His refuge, and should have confidence in Allah's promise about tribulation: ﴾*We shall surely try you, till We make evident those of you who strive hard and have patience, and till We test your record*﴿ [47:31]; ﴾*Think you to enter Paradise when there has not yet befallen you that which befell those who passed away before you?*﴿ [2:214]; ﴾*Alif Lām Mīm. Do the people reckon that they will be left to say, 'We believe', without being tested?*﴿ [29:2].

The Shaykh alludes to this with his next words: *For* ﴾*the believers have been tried, and mightily shaken; and lo, the hypocrites and those with sickness in their hearts say: Allah and His Messenger have promised us nothing but delusion*﴿ [33:11–12]. The Shaykh quotes these words here as a form of justification for his request for protection, and a confession of the dire state he is in, wherein the soul displays symptoms of the sickness hidden in the heart, which leads one to think ill of Allah. This is just what happened to the hypocrites at the Battle of the Trench, when the enemy beset them from all sides, and their eyes were startled, and their hearts were in their mouths, and those with misgivings in their hearts thought all kinds of thoughts about Allah. Here the believers were tried, and mightily shaken, and what was in the hearts of the hypocrites was manifested on their tongues when they said, *Allah and His Messenger have promised us nothing but delusion.* Likewise, what was in the hearts of the believers was manifested on their tongues when they said, ﴾*'This is what Allah and His Messenger promised us, and Allah and His Messenger spoke true!' And it only increased them in faith and resignation*﴿ [33:22].

The Shaykh رضي الله عنه is saying, as it were: 'I only asked for protection through fear of being sent astray by the tribulation that all believers must endure so that the wheat can be separated from the chaff; for there is no protector from Allah's command, save for those on whom He has mercy.' This is an expression of concern for faith, which is one's capital and the foundation of all one's deeds. Allah says: ﴾*Whoso seeks protection from Allah has been guided to a straight path*﴿ [3:101].

Now different copies of the Litany give these words in different ways; some give it just as it appears in the Qur'an, as *And lo, the hypocrites and those with sickness in their hearts say…*, followed by a rejoinder to their statement. Other copies give it as 'so that the hypocrites…will say…', according to the meaning intended here, which is to show that the plea and the tribulation [of the believers] lead on to further tribulation [of the hypocrites]. In that case, it does not mean the same as it does in the Qur'an but instead shows why the verse is being quoted in this context, namely that of extolling Allah's blessings. This is the correct version as I have seen it in the handwriting of Sidi Abū ʿAbdallāh Muḥammad ibn ʿAbbād (may Allah have mercy on him).

So make us steadfast, give us victory, and subject to us this sea, as You subjected the sea to Moses عليه السلام, the fire to Abraham عليه السلام, the mountains and iron to David عليه السلام, the wind and demons and jinn to Solomon عليه السلام.

These words refer back to what has just been said, in successive order: *Make us steadfast* at times when we might slip, times of difficulty and danger; and *give us victory* over our enemies, the hypocrites and those with sickness in their hearts; *and subject to us this sea* that we are in, wherein we are exposed to all that. Subject it to us in a way that nullifies all that might be feared, and brings forth all that might be hoped for.

It might also be said: *Make us firm* in faith, *give us victory* with certitude, and *subject to us* the *sea* of our life in this world and this religion, so that we are saved from doubts, suppositions and fancies, and so that we are aided by the inner realities of faith and surrender; for one of the signs of divine aid is that one preserves his faith in the divine Oneness at times of trial, as Sidi Abū ʿAlī al-Daqqāq said.

The metaphor of the 'subjection' is drawn from its aspect of facilitation and generosity, and is not meant to suggest exact equivalency; for this subjection was a gift and a kindness from Allah, and therefore was a means of strengthening faith as well as a display of kindness.

He *subjected the sea to Moses* عليه السلام twice, first by giving him salvation when his mother cast him into it, and then again by giving him salvation [when parting it for him] and destroying those who belied him, and drowning his enemies.

He subjected *the fire to Abraham* عليه السلام by making it cool and harmless for him.

He subjected *the mountains to David* عليه السلام by making them hymn the praises of their Lord alongside him by night and by dawn, and subjected *the iron* to him by making it malleable for him and for those who were with him, so that they could fashion armour from it as easily as if it were dough.

He subjected *the wind to Solomon* عليه السلام so that he could command it on journeys that lasted as long as a month away and a month back. Allah says: ﴾*And of the demons, some dived for him and did other work besides*﴿ [21:82]; indeed Allah ﷻ tells us that ﴾*They fashioned for him whatsoever he would – places of worship, statues, porringers like water-troughs, and anchored cooking-pots*﴿ [34:13]. Demons [*shayāṭīn*] are a kind of jinn who do no good works whatsoever, nor have any propensity for it; they are the opposite of angels. The Shaykh mentions them before the jinn here by way of mentioning the general before the specific; and Allah and His Messenger ﷺ know best.

Subject to us every sea You possess, in the earth and the sky,
the kingdom and the dominion, the sea of this life
and the sea of the life to come. Subject to us everything,
O You in whose hand is dominion of everything!

The request for the subjection of every sea in the earth and the sky is an expression of neediness for all things, and in all things; it is a realisation of poverty before Allah in every state. They have said about this:

With every breath, I am in need of You,
Even if my brow is furnished with a crown.

Concerning *the kingdom and the dominion*, the kingdom [*mulk*] is the physical world, which can be perceived by the senses and the mind; and the dominion [*malakūt*] is the unseen subtle world, which can be perceived by the intellect and understanding.

So we have specific language following general, and then general following specific; this alludes to the greatness of divine lordship and the reality of human servitude. It is a way of making the greatest request possible, in accordance with the Prophet's ﷺ words '*When you ask of Allah, make great the request; for nothing is too much for Allah.*'[73] They said, 'In that case we will ask for more, O Messenger of Allah!' He replied, '*Allah has even more*' [*Allāhu akthar*], or '*Allah is even greater*' [*Allāhu akbar*].

In this supplication, the Shaykh has adhered to the proper etiquette of personal prayer, asking for individual things before

73 Numerous *Ṣaḥīḥ* hadith with similar wordings can be found in the various collections.

multiple things. Master Abū al-Qāsim al-Qushayrī رضي الله عنه said: 'Asking for too much puts a lock on the door.' Good things should be asked for one after another. A group of prisoners of war were once brought to a ruler, who commanded that they all be executed. One of them said to him, 'By Him who gave you what you have, would you not be kind enough to give us a drink of water?' He assented, and they were given water. Once they had drunk, they said to him, 'By Him who gave you what you have, do not kill your guests!' He commanded that they be set free, saying: 'Have mercy on anyone who can draw even a single tear from your eye!'

This is why the supplications in the Qur'an are usually short and grouped together. Indeed, the longest supplications it contains are seven verses at the end of *Sūrat al-Baqara* and five in *Sūrat Āl 'Imrān*, and there are no longer prayers than those in any one place in it. Take note of this.

Other etiquettes of personal prayer are to ask for those things which are most pertinent to the occasion, and to ask for what is needed most before what is needed least, as the Shaykh رضي الله عنه does here. Another is to avoid asking for anything impossible, whether by law, reason or custom. Qarāfī[74] mentioned several issues pertaining to this and discussed them, including the common prayer 'forgive all the Muslims and believers', giving several explanations for why such a prayer is valid, at greater length than can be quoted here.

Concerning the several seas of which the Shaykh رضي الله عنه speaks, they differ according to the material and the spiritual. This makes it clear that by 'sea', he means every enormous thing that contains

74 Shihāb al-Dīn al-Qarāfī was a Mālikī *faqīh* considered one of the greatest scholars of his time. He wrote a number of influential works d.684AH/1285CE

benefits and harms, whether it be material or spiritual. It has been said that there is a sea in the sky, a sea under the earth, and a sea between the sky and the earth; and that this sea of ours is the saliva of a whale, and that it sits in the hollow of an angel's thumb. Ibn al-Ṭallāʿ related this among some uncommon hadiths, and added ones stating that Shuʿayb ﷺ lived for three thousand years and had twelve thousand dogs among his herds, and that Allah raised the Prophet's ﷺ parents from the dead and they believed in him.

Concerning the kingdom [*mulk*] and the dominion [*malakūt*], as we said previously, the *mulk* is the physical world, which can be perceived by the senses and the mind; and the *malakūt* is the unseen subtle world, which can be perceived by the intellect and understanding.

Concerning *the sea of this life and the sea of the life to come*, this means the sea that is this world, and the sea that is the hereafter. They are both enormous and vast; indeed, they are the greatest of all seas, and they contain both physical and spiritual realities; and they cannot be traversed without Allah's subjection of them, so one must turn back to Allah in order to traverse them.

The reason he says *O You in whose hand is dominion* [malakūt] *of everything*, and does not mention the *mulk*, is that it is enough to mention the stronger of them; for He who possesses the spiritual realm necessarily possesses the material realm, and not vice versa; and Allah knows best.

Kāf Ha Yā ʿAyn Ṣād

The scholars differ over the meaning of the disconnected Arabic letters which open certain chapters of the Qur'an. Some say that they are among the allegorical passages whose meaning is known only to Allah. Ibn al-Subkī said that Allah might reveal their meaning to some of those who He elects for this knowledge. It has been said that they are the seals of the Lord of the Worlds and His symbols in His Book, or that they are the Supreme Name of Allah, or that they represent the number of the Muḥammadan nations and how long each will last.

The soundest opinion on the subject is that they are symbols whose true meaning is known only to Him who put them there; and the different ways they have been understood does not mean that they do not have meanings that no man can know.

Now one way of understanding them is that they represent the themes of the chapters which contain them; and it seems that this is what the Shaykh intended by them here; and Allah knows best. There are five letters here: *kāf* for sufficiency [*kifāya*], *hā* for guidance [*hidāya*], *yā* for patronage [*wilāya*], *ʿayn* for care [*ʿināya*] and *ṣād* for faithfulness [*ṣidq*]. These five words are all manifested in the stories which this chapter[75] contains. See how He sufficed Zachariah by giving him an heir to whom to pass on his patronage, and guided him to prayer, and answered his plea after he acknowledged his inability to heal his wife's condition, giving him a son despite his weakness; and He manifested His care for him, his wife and his child in all that for which He was their patron. He then did the same for Mary and her child, and Abraham and his children, and Moses and his brother; and He bestowed His favour on Enoch (Idrīs), Noah, and the other prophets – peace be upon them all. To explain this in detail would take too long.

75 Meaning *Sūrah Maryam* (19), which begins with these letters.

Understanding by means of the insightful recognition of symbols is more complete than understanding by word-for-word explanation. Thus the Shaykh mentions these letters here by way of seeking sufficiency, guidance, patronage, care and a fulfilling of the promise for an answer to his prayer for the aforementioned subjection, in a way that is unfettered by boundaries or limits; and such a thing can only be alluded to by means of symbols. He asks that these things be granted as perfectly as they were to those he mentioned before when he said *as You subjected the sea to Moses...*

The letters could also represent certain of the divine Names: the Sufficient [*al-Kāfī*], the Guide [*al-Hādī*], the Patron [*al-Walī*], the Great [*al-ʿAẓīm*] and He who Fulfils His Promise [*al-Ṣādiq Waʿdah*].

It could well be that the letters symbolise both of these at the same time, which is an acknowledgement of the vastness of their meanings and the power of their effect on the soul; this also conforms to the way that the Mighty Book always consigns the secret to Allah alone.

The Shaykh repeats these letters three times, either to signify his wish that the things he seeks be granted to his body, heart and spirit; or that they be granted outwardly, inwardly and both of them together; or that they be granted in the present, the past and the future. It may also refer to matters of separation, matters of connection, and matters which share the two aspects. This depends on how the individual mind understands it, according to its aptitude; and this broader viewpoint is how the people of knowledge go about teaching others.

Some people have approached this question from the perspective of the numerical values of the letters[76] and their

76 Every Arabic letter has a numerical value (known as '*abjad*').

peculiar attributes, and what can be deduced from this; others have suggested that there is a secret that cannot be understood or touched by human perception. The former approach is blessed and useful, and it inspires powerful aspirations; the second is of little use, since it closes the door to understanding.

That is all the pen will allow me to write on the matter; it belongs to Allah alone, whom we ask for peace.

Give us victory, for You are the best who give victory.
Clear our vision, for You are the best who clear visions.
Forgive us, for You are the best of forgivers.
Have mercy on us, for You are the best of the merciful.
Give us sustenance, for You are the best of providers.
Guide us, and save us from the wrongdoing folk.
Give us a goodly wind, as may be in Your knowledge; loose it upon us from the storehouses of Your mercy; and carry us upon it in honour, with safety and wellbeing in our religion, in our life in this world, and in the world to come. Truly, You have power over all things.

This is an expansion of the subjection which is being sought, just as the previous words were a symbol and a general allusion to it. This passage gives detail, and then explains that detail. To give victory is an aspect of sufficiency; to give clear vision is an aspect of guidance; to provide sustenance is an aspect of patronage; mercy and guidance are an aspect of care; to save is an aspect of faithfulness to a promise; and Allah says: ﴾*It was ever incumbent upon Us to give victory to the believers*﴿ [30:47].

The mention of the *goodly wind* is a return to the need at hand.[77] That it be a 'goodly' wind, and not just any wind, is essential, since otherwise it might be destructive. Indeed, every time the word 'wind' is used in the singular in the Qur'an, it means a destructive wind, unless it is qualified as in His words ﴾[*The ships*] *carry them with a goodly wind*﴿ [10:22]; on the other hand, He says: ﴾*...and then comes a stormy wind*﴿ [10:22]. Understand this.

His words *as may be in Your knowledge* avoid making the request specific, leaving it up to Allah to specify. He is saying, as it were: 'Whatever goodly wind is in Your knowledge, give it to us, whether it corresponds to what we know or not; for no one knows what is truly good but You.' We might love something even though it is bad for us, or hate something even though it is good for us.

We once experienced this when we were at sea and the winds failed. Some of us hoped for a powerful wind because they believed it would be for the best, but we were ill at ease with their suggestion for the reasons we have just explained; and perhaps I even told them not to ask for it. In the end, Allah sent wind that was so powerful it almost drowned us, and would have done so had it not abated at the last minute. This made them come to their senses and ask for a wind that was goodly, in whatever way, and sure enough we got what we needed and completed our journey safely.

The Shaykh رضي الله عنه then says: *Loose it upon us from the storehouses of Your mercy.* That is, make it blow upon us with mercy, and from a merciful source, not with wrath, or from a wrathful source; for Allah might have mercy with something that is a torment in the short run, or deal torment with something that seems merciful

77 Since it pertains to travel by sea.

in the short run. Allah destroyed the people of ʿĀd with wind, yet subjected the wind to Solomon عليه السلام, so that it was a divine favour in his kingdom; and He looses it upon land and sea alike. Thus it is with all of those things which Allah sets loose: they bear His mercy to some, and His punishment to others. If they are sent from a merciful source, they are a blessing; and if they are sent from a wrathful source, they are a curse. Therefore the Prophet ﷺ would say, whenever the wind blew a gale: *'O Allah, do not destroy us with Your wrath and Your punishment! Have mercy upon us before that!'*

The Shaykh's request here might also simply be for mercy in any form, without any particular means or cause.

His رضي الله عنه words *And carry us upon it in honour, with safety and wellbeing in our religion, in our life in this world, and in the world to come* mean: 'Carry us upon the sea with this wind with the same honour with which You carried Adam and his progeny, and Noah and his progeny; for You said, and Your word is the truth: ﴾*We honoured the progeny of Adam, and carried them on land and sea, and provided them with goodly sustenance, and favoured them greatly over many of those We created*﴿ [17:70].'

By asking to be carried with honour, he seeks to avoid being carried with the humiliation that was dealt to the people of ʿĀd in the form of a wind so strong it carried even their camels away; Allah says: ﴾*It spared naught that it reached, but made it all as dust*﴿ [51:22].

Safety means the dispelling of all obstacles and threats, so that neither evil nor harm can assail one. *Wellbeing* means that the present moment is free of worry and difficulty. If it is attained by contentment and resignation to Allah, then it is perfect wellbeing; and if it attained by the utilisation of the appropriate means, then it is ordinary wellbeing.

Safety in religion is attained by adherence to its commandments, and by yielding to its authority without any hesitation or opposition. Safety in the life of this world is attained by meeting one's goals in the right way, and avoiding the obstacles that stand in front of them. When all this is combined, one lives in happiness and contentment; for the affairs of this life and the next cannot be perfect without happiness. This is true even for the denizens of Paradise: Allah says to them ﴾*Eat and drink happily*﴿ [52:19], and were it not for the word 'happily', theirs would not be a blessed state.

The Shaykh's ﵁ words *Truly, You have power over all things* mean: 'This is not difficult for You, and it is not beyond Your power to give it to me, without any means or cause.' This evokes the helplessness of servitude and the infinitude of lordship, and Allah's power to withhold, give, facilitate, and so on.

O Allah, give us ease in our affairs, with peace for our hearts and bodies, and safety and wellbeing in our worldly life and our religion. Be our companion in our travels, and keep watch over our families in our stead. Blot out the faces of our enemies, and fix them where they stand, so they can neither move nor reach us. ﴾Had We willed, We would have blotted out their eyes; and they would race to the path, but how should they see? Or had We willed, We would have fixed them where they stood, so they neither could go forward, nor return﴿.

After asking for safety and wellbeing in the religion, the life of this world and the life of the world to come, the Shaykh ﵁ now asks for ease in the affairs thereof, since the former does not necessarily entail the latter, and whilst the latter is of no value without the former. None of this is of any value unless there is peace for the heart and the body.

The reason he mentioned the life of this world before that of the next world is that safety and wellbeing in this world are required in order to win the good life of the hereafter and its perfect boons; for there can be no perfection, nor any peace from the distractions and worries of the soul, as long as one has an imbalanced nature. One must have knowledge, intelligence and life at all times and in all situations. Because of this, Ibn ʿAṭāʾ Allāh says in the *Ḥikam*: 'It is a perfect blessing when He provides you with what suffices you, and withholds from you what would cause you to go astray, so that you have little to rejoice in and little to grieve over.'

The reason why the Messenger of Allah ﷺ asked his Lord to give him his sustenance little by little was so that he would never be worried by dearth, or distracted by excess. May Allah have mercy on Abū ʿAlī al-Thaqafī ؓ, who said: 'Fie to the distractions of this world when they are present, and to the grief they cause when they are absent! An intelligent mind does not put any value in things which cause distraction when they are present, and grief when they are absent.' They have said about this:

He who praises the world for its pleasure
    Will soon, upon my life, be cursing it!
When it goes, a man grieves for its loss;
    When it comes, it brings much strife with it.

Some of those who have recited this litany have gone out of their way to change it, putting *religion* before *worldly life* and adding, 'and our hereafter and our souls.' This is not authentic in terms of the narration, nor is it fitting in terms of wisdom, even if it seemed that way to the mind of the person who added it. Perhaps he also claimed that it was narrated to him this way, which would be to add the sin of lying to this unsanctioned alteration – may Allah be our refuge from this!

The Shaykh ﵁ then says: *Be our companion in our travels, and keep watch over our families in our stead.* That is, may we not be wronged or harmed, and may goodness flow through what we have left behind as though we have brought it with us. These words are derived from the prayer of the Prophet ﷺ: *'O Allah, You are the companion in travel, and the one who watches over the family.'*[78] The 'one who watches over' [*khalīfa*] is the one who takes care of things after being appointed for this duty. The 'companion' [*ṣāḥib*] is he who stays close to one, guiding one to benefit and protecting one from harm. When the word is used to refer to the Creator, it means sufficiency and guardianship by way of increased mercy, aid, bestowal of benefit and protection from harm. Were it not that the Lawgiver ﷺ himself used these words, it would not be appropriate for anyone to call Him by them; He used them in order to make the concept easier for human minds to understand. The scholars then differed as to whether these terms are allowed to be used by anyone else, taking into consideration the meaning and the conventional use of the terms, and whether or not their use would cause confusion. Reflect on this, and take note of it.

The Shaykh's ﵁ words *Blot out the faces of our enemies* mean: Turn their faces around to face backward, so that they cannot act in the way they wish to, nor in any useful way. Allah says: ﴾*...Before We blot out faces, and turn them in upon their backs*﴿ [4:47]; He

78 Narrated by Muslim (*Ṣaḥīḥ*, *al-Ḥajj*, 2392).

made the words 'turn them in upon their backs' serve to explain what 'blot out' means. Consult the works of exegesis for more on this.

As for his words *and fix them where they stand*, this means: 'Make them too weak to move from their places, so that they cannot move elsewhere nor come to us; this means that everyone else will be safe from them, as we are.'

The Shaykh ﵁ then quotes verses wherein this obliteration, fixing and covering are all mentioned: ﴾*Had We willed, We would have blotted out their eyes; and they would race to the path, but how should they see? Or had We willed, We would have fixed them where they stood, so they neither could go forward, nor return*﴿ [36:66–67].

The reason he recites this verses right after praying for what they contain is to affirm that such a thing may happen, support his request for it, and seek the blessing of the verses in the hope that what they describe will be applied to his enemies. It is also an allusion to the fact that such an occurrence is a special property of these verses; for the special property of every invocation is found in its meaning, and its application is found in its import, and its secret is found in its number. This is the approach taken by all, or most, of those who have spoken on the subject of special properties by way of analogy and meditative discourse, such as al-Qāḍī al-Tamīmī, Shaykh Abū al-ʿAbbās al-Būnī, and others; and Allah knows best.

We have already seen the meaning of blotting out and fixing in place. When the eyes are blotted out, their owners are unable to see, and they look for the path but cannot find it; and even if they do find it, they cannot reach it; and even if they do reach it, they cannot traverse it. They are prevented from doing so in any case, since their sight is blotted out and they are fixed where they stand, so *how should they see?*

﴾*Yā Sīn. By the Wise Qur'an, truly you are of the messengers, upon a straight path. This is a revelation of the Almighty, the Merciful; that you might warn a people whose forefathers were not warned, so they heed not. Already has sentence been passed against most of them, so they believe not. Verily, We have placed shackles on their necks, even up to the chins, so they bend not. And We have placed a barrier before them, and a barrier behind them, and enshrouded them, so that they see not.*﴿

The Shaykh ﷺ then returns to the start of the same chapter, *Sūrat Yā Sīn*. The reason the Shaykh recites these verses is that the secret of the opening two letters flows throughout the whole chapter; the chapter revolves around its opening. The first two letters symbolise the themes around which the chapter revolves, namely patronage [*wilāya*] and safety [*salāma*], and the manifestation of His Name 'Patron' [*al-Walī*] after 'Peace' [*al-Salām*]. The explanation of this is that after the letters, He then begins by swearing upon the Wise Qur'an that he ﷺ is truly of the messengers, upon a straight path, and that this straight path is a revelation of the Almighty, who does not allow those under His patronage to be debased, and the Merciful, who gives peace to all under His patronage. He then affirms that the purpose of this is to warn a people who have never been warned, nor had their forefathers before them, so that they are a heedless people. This is a warning and a caution for those whom Allah wishes to benefit; otherwise, *already has sentence been passed against most of them, so they believe not*. Those who believe and respond are the minority, for whom Allah wills kindness. Thus these words are a pronouncement of the peace and patronage He has given to His Prophet ﷺ, and to those of His servants who believe.

If you then continue to the end of the chapter, you will find that it follows these same themes, united in both its inner secret and its outer form, until it ends with His words ﴾*Glory be to Him who has dominion over all things, and to whom you shall return!*﴿ [36:83].

Indeed, everything in the Qur'an revolves around the aforementioned patronage and peace, inasmuch as this is its intention. This is why the noble hadith says: *'The heart of the Qur'an is Yā Sīn'*, as is narrated by Tirmidhī[79] and others. It has been said that the heart of *Yā Sīn* in turn is ﴾*Peace; a word from a Merciful Lord. Now keep yourselves apart on this Day, you sinners*﴿ [36:58–59]. Reflect on this; and all success is from Allah.

Now if you ask why the Shaykh quotes the verses from the middle of the chapter and then goes back and quotes the opening verses of it, my answer is that he quotes the first verses independently, and then quotes the opening of the chapter as a reminder, as it were, showing that the passages have a common meaning, and that one may take from it all according to one's intention. There is nothing wrong with quoting passages separately in this way, as long as the intention is not to change the order, and as long as no one would infer that the order has been changed; and Allah knows best.

79 *Al-Jāmiʿ al-Ṣaḥīḥ, Faḍā'il al-Qur'ān*, 2812.

Disfigured be those faces!
﴾*And faces shall be humbled before the Eternal Living, the All-Sustaining; while whoever bears wrongdoing shall have failed.*﴿

Disfigured be those faces means may they be humbled, debased and despoiled, so that they fail to attain their desire and are defeated. The Messenger of Allah ﷺ spoke these words on the day of Uḥud when he encountered the enemy army after the Muslims had scattered from around him, thinking that he had been slain after Satan's cry had been taken up. He ﷺ took a handful of pebbles and threw them at the faces of the enemy, crying, *'Disfigured be those faces!'* Every one of them was hit in the eyes, and they turned their heels and fled as he ﷺ looked on, saying:

I am the Prophet, no lie!
I am the scion of ʿAbd al-Muṭṭalib!

Allah ﷻ then revealed about this: ﴾*You threw not when you threw, but it was Allah that threw*﴿ [8:17]. Thus these words are connected to the defeat of armies and the banishment of enemies, seeking blessing from the Sunna. The Shaykh continues this by then quoting another verse pertaining to the banishment and obliteration of enemies, pleading for victory in every way: ﴾*And faces shall be humbled* [*ʿanat*] *before the Eternal Living, the All-Sustaining*﴿ [20:111]. This proclaims that the subjects of these words are all miserable creatures, for *ʿanat* means to be abased and humiliated.

The Eternal Living, the All-Sustaining is Allah ﷻ; for He lives and does not die, whilst all else that lives must die; the life of things that die is only borrowed, and has no reality save through the

Living, who dies not. The truly Living is Allah ﷻ, whilst all else has no life even if it is alive, since next to Him it is virtually dead, and can only move through Him; and although it seems to have power, its power has no effect.

The All-Sustaining [*al-Qayyūm*] is He who sustains Himself and needs nothing, and who sustains all other things, so that everything needs Him for its sustenance. He is also the One who ﴾*sees to* [*al-Qā'im 'alā*] *every soul for what it has earned*﴿; that is, the One who requites them for their actions. *The Eternal Living* and *the All-Sustaining* are among the Greatest Names, the Names of the Holy Essence. It is said that together they constitute the Supreme Name of Allah; and this is both suggested by hadiths and attested to by inner realities. A hadith of Asmā' bint 'Umays ﵂ says: *'The Supreme Name of Allah is in Āl 'Imrān and al-Baqara.'* Other narrations add *'and Ṭā Hā'.*[80] The author of *al-Silāḥ* said, 'It is His Name "The Eternal Living, the All-Sustaining", because these chapters only have this in common.' However, the former narration could suggest that it refers to ﴾*Your God is One God; there is no god besides Him, the Compassionate, the Merciful*﴿ [2:163] and the opening of *Sūrat Āl 'Imrān*. It is also noteworthy that one of our shaykhs said in a letter he wrote to a jurist, *'Allah, there is no god besides Him, the Eternal Living, the All-Sustaining. In the Name of Allah, the Compassionate, the Merciful, Alif-Lām-Mīm, Allah, there is no god besides Him, the Eternal Living, the All-Sustaining* and *And faces shall be humbled before the Eternal Living, the All-Sustaining* are the encompassments of the hidden Supreme Name.' They encompass it in the sense of the aforementioned narration that 'Every Name whose meaning is found in all the other Names...', so reflect on this.

80 Ibn Mājah narrated it on the authority of Abū Umāma (*Sunan, al-Du'ā'*, 3846), as did al-Ṭabarānī (*Kabīr*, 6759).

The Shaykh ﷺ then continues the quote: ﴾*... while whoever bears wrongdoing shall have failed*﴿ [20:111]. That is, they will have failed in this world by losing out on victory and divine aid, and they will have failed in the hereafter by being rejected and submitted to grievous punishment. They are promised failure in both lives, and nothing they gain will be of any benefit to them. Allah will continue to punish one wrongdoer by means of another until He has punished them all, as He says: ﴾*Thus We let some of the wrongdoers have power over others, because of what they are wont to earn*﴿ [6:129].

All this is implied by the verse, which the Shaykh ﷺ quotes here as an invocation, all the while thinking the best of Allah; it constitutes a prayer that they fail in their scheme. Note this, and understand it.

Ṭā Sīn.
Ḥā Mīm, ʿAyn Sīn Qāf.
﴾*He has loosed the two seas; they come together, but between them is a barrier they do not cross.*﴿
Ḥā Mīm, Ḥā Mīm, Ḥā Mīm, Ḥā Mīm, Ḥā Mīm, Ḥā Mīm, Ḥā Mīm.
The matter is done, the victory come.
Against us they shall not be helped.
﴾*Ḥā Mīm. The revelation of the Book from Allah, the Almighty, the All-Knowing: Forgiver of Sins, Accepter of Repentance, Terrible in Punishment, Infinite in Bounty: no god is there but He; unto Him is the final becoming.*﴿

These are symbols by which blessing is sought, in the same

allegorical way as we have seen in the case of *Kāf Hā Yā ʿAyn Ṣād* and *Yā Sīn*, Allah willing. The *ṭā* is for purity [*ṭahāra*], the *sīn* for safety [*salāma*], the *ḥā mīm* for protection [*ḥimāya*], the *ʿayn* for concern [*ʿināya*], the *sīn* for safety [*salāma*], the *qāf* for power [*qudra*]. The stories of *Sūrat al-Naml* [which begins with these letters] tell of the purity and safety of the believers, and the same for the rest of what is related in it. This begins with the purity of Moses عليه السلام and his safety from Pharaoh and his hordes; then there is the safety of the kingdom of Solomon عليه السلام and David عليه السلام from flaw, tyranny and negligence; then the safety of the hoopoe and its purity from disobedience;[81] then the safety of Balqīs and her purity in surrender to Allah, and the safety of Solomon's عليه السلام army and their purity when encountering her people; then the purity of Ṣāliḥ عليه السلام and his safety from his people; then the purity of Hūd عليه السلام and his safety from the deeds and harms of his people; then the purity of Allah's sincere servants, and the peace He gives them.

Apply the same to the rest of the chapter, and then see how the secret of dominion [*al-mulk*] is manifest here, whilst it is symbolised by the letter *mīm* in those chapters which begin *Ṭā Sīn Mīm*. The letter *mīm* is not needed here, since its meaning is clearly manifest, and symbols are only needed for those things which are subtle, so that the symbol brings out the secret. This is why *Sūrat al-Tawba* does not begin with the *Basmala*, as a sign that it is characterised by a mercy that is not found in other chapters, namely how the Real reaches out to His servants by buying their souls,[82] and how He gives them a clear description of the people of

81 See Qur'an 27:20, where the Hoopoe bird brings tidings of the Queen of Sheba (Balqīs) to Solomon عليه السلام.

82 Allusion to ﴾*Allah has bought from the believers their selves and their possessions against the gift of Paradise*﴿ [9:111].

falsehood so that they do not fall prey to their traps and obstacles. Apply the same thing to the chapters which begin *Ḥā Mīm*, and reflect on what this means.

Consider also His words ﴾*Ḥā Mīm, ʿAyn Sīn Qāf*﴿ [42:1–2]: *Ḥā Mīm* is for protection, which is why the Messenger of Allah ﷺ said to the Companions on the day of Uḥud: *'Let your battle cry be: Ḥā Mīm, they shall not be victorious!'*[83] Allah defends those who believe. This was given further interpretation by their words 'Allah is our Patron, and you have no patron!', in answer to the taunt of the idolaters 'We have 'Uzzā,[84] and you have no 'Uzzā!' And to the idolaters' cry 'Elevate Hubal',[85] they answered: 'Allah is higher and greater still!'

The letters *ʿAyn Sīn Qāf* represent His Names the All-Knowing [*al-ʿAlīm*], the All-Hearing [*al-Samīʿ*] and the All-Sustaining [*al-Qayyūm*]. So there is concern along with protection, safety and sustenance; for protection is to be hoped from His knowledge, His gift of peace and His power. Protection pertains to the presence of the divine Acts, while what has been said about the letters *ʿAyn Sīn Qāf* pertains to the meanings of the divine Qualities. They are *two seas* flowing through creation that mix in their affects but not in their realities, for *between them is a barrier.* Action and reaction *do not cross* and thus resemble one another. That is, their meanings enter the realms of majesty and beauty, yet between them is a barrier they do not cross: the one does not infringe upon the other and thus nullify it.

The Shaykh then invokes the seven instances of *Ḥā Mīm*; they

83 Narrated by al-Tirmidhī (*Jāmiʿ, al-Jihād*, 1605) and Abū Dāwūd (*Sunan, al-Jihād*, 2230).

84 A pagan idol.

85 Another idol.

are seven in number because seven protections are necessary, differing in their origin, their branches, their area and their extent, according to the different ways they are manifested. The explanation of the first of them is summarised in Allah's words ﴾*Ḥā Mīm. The revelation of the Book from Allah, the Almighty, the All-Knowing: Forgiver of Sins, Accepter of Repentance, Terrible in Punishment, Infinite in Bounty: no god is there but He; unto Him is the final becoming*﴿ [40:1–3].

So each letter represents the teachings of its chapter and the themes of its stories, and the like. Every chapter of the *Ḥā Mīms* has a universal point, and a clear defining verse. His might and knowledge are manifested in the first of them, whose central point is ﴾*We shall indeed give victory to Our messengers...*﴿ [40:51], and which ends with ﴾*The Way of Allah, which has ever taken course for His servants; and then the disbelievers will be ruined*﴿ [40:85].

His forgiveness and compassion are manifested in the second of them, *Sūrat Fuṣṣilat*, which begins with mercy: ﴾*Ḥā Mīm. A revelation from the Compassionate, the Merciful*﴿ [41:1], has its central point in ﴾*Naught is said to you but what already was said to the messengers before you. Your Lord is a Lord of forgiveness, and of painful retribution*﴿ [41:43], and ends with His words ﴾*Suffices it not as to your Lord, that He is witness over everything? Are they not in doubt touching the encounter with their Lord? Does He not encompass everything?*﴿ [41:53–54].

His willingness to accept repentance and give pardon is manifested in the third of them, *Sūrat al-Shūrā*, which opens with an affirmation that He is High and Great, has its central point in ﴾*It is He who accepts repentance from His servants, and pardons evil deeds; He knows the things you do*﴿ [42:25], and ends with His words ﴾*And surely you shall guide unto a straight path*﴿ [42:52].

The fourth, *Sūrat al-Zukhruf,* contains a manifestation of His requital and punishment of the disbelievers. Consider this, given how the chapter begins with His words ﴿*How many a prophet We sent among the ancients*﴾ [43:6] up to His words ﴿*We destroyed men stronger in valour than they, and the example of the ancients passed away*﴾ [43:8], has its central point in the description of how the denizens of Hell will be punished and how they will cry out ﴿*Let your Lord have done with us!*﴾ [43:77] and so forth, and how it ends with His words ﴿*Yet pardon them, and say, 'Peace!' Soon they will know*﴾ [43:89].

His great bounty and goodness is then manifested at the start of the fifth chapter, *Sūrat al-Dukhān*, which begins with His words ﴿*Therein all wisdom is distinguished*﴾ [44:5], has its central point in ﴿*The Day of Decision shall be their appointed time, all together*﴾ [44:40]; and from there to the end of the chapter, the description of His bounty and might is clear.

Godhood and its proofs are manifested in *Sūrat al-Jāthiya,* which begins with a call for contemplation, centres on ﴿*Then We set you upon an open way of the Command; therefore follow it*﴾ [45:18] and ends with His words ﴿*So to Allah be praise, the Lord of the heavens, the Lord of the earth, the Lord of the Worlds. His is the dominion of the heavens and the earth; He is the Almighty, the Wise*﴾ [45:36–37].

He ﷻ then declares that all things shall return to Him in *Sūrat al-Aḥqāf,* which starts with the beginning of creation and its return to Him, and then speaks of their existence and their affairs, and then ends with His words ﴿*Shall any be destroyed, but the wicked?*﴾ [46:35].

Reflect on this, and behold it with the eye of your heart, and you will find that it is perfectly profound in a way that I cannot express; none can express it save those who possess true hearts and true vision, and those of contemplation and profundity; and our Lord is the Opener, the All-Knowing.

He then continues: *The matter is done*, that is, it was difficult, and then became balanced, and then continued with protection; *the victory come*, that is, the help of the divine power has come. *Against us they shall not be helped*; he is speaking about the enemies and all who resemble them.

The Shaykh ﷺ then quotes the opening verses of *Sūrat al-Mu'min*. A noble hadith says: *'Whoso recites Āyat al-Kursī and the opening of Ḥā Mīm* [*al-Mu'min*] *in the morning will be protected until the evening; and whoso recites it in the evening will be protected until the morning.'* Another narration adds *Sūrat al-Dukhān*. We have already spoken about this chapter above, so reflect on it as best you can; and all success is from Allah.

Bismi'Llāh is our door,
Tabāraka our walls,
Yā Sīn our roof,
Kāf Hā Yā 'Ayn Ṣād our sufficiency,
Ḥā Mīm, 'Ayn Sīn Qāf our protection.
Allah will suffice you against them,
and He is the All-Hearing, the All-Knowing.

The Shaykh is saying: In the Name of Allah we enter all our affairs, and exit them; and behind it we take refuge from every blight and trial; for the door is the entrance, and the barrier to every blight and trial. The *Basmala* is the door to all things, and the key to them as well. A hadith says: *'Whoso wishes to live happily and die a martyr, let him say In the Name of Allah when beginning all things, and Praise be to Allah when finishing them.'* Allah ﷻ commanded us to invoke His Name when beginning things, sometimes with the complete *Basmala* formula [*In the Name of Allah, the Compassionate, the Merciful*], and sometimes with the shorter form [*In the Name of Allah*].

So the *Basmala* is the door, and *Tabāraka* (that is, *Sūrat Tabārak*) is the walls, because it is a fortress from enemies and a storehouse of benefits, as has been said about it; and because it is a source of reliance, strength in debate, and protection for all who seek blessing by reciting it. They say that it was the wont of Shaykh Abū Madyan ﵁ to recite it, and that he would associate it with the invocation *There is no god but Allah, alone with no partner; His is all dominion, and His is all praise, and He is able to do all things*, and would read it in his solitary vigils. *Sūrat al-Nās* also shares the same meaning; and Allah knows best.

Yā Sīn is the roof, which provides cover and shelter from things that fall from above; so *Sūrat Yā Sīn* is a cover and a guard for those who recite it.

We have already seen the meaning and significance of *Kāf Hā Yā ʿAyn Ṣād*, and how each letter represents a Name whose theme it signifies, and how its secret is in its number. We have also seen the meaning of *Ḥā Mīm, ʿAyn Sīn Qāf*, and how it means protection, care, safety and sustenance.

It has been said that if one interlocks his fingers when saying *Kāf Hā Yā ʿAyn Ṣād, Ḥā Mīm ʿAyn Sīn Qāf*, intending each letter to represent a finger, and then goes to see someone whom he fears and opens his fingers in his presence when he meets him, whether or not the person sees him, he will be given protection and great success. If he adds to this *Allah will suffice you against them, and*

He is the All-Hearing, the All-Knowing, a wonderful secret will be given to him. This is why the Shaykh ﷺ invokes it here; for it contains the secret of reliance and sufficiency. He repeats it three times because the Sunna of invocation is to repeat things three times; and Allah knows best.

The veil of the Throne has been dropped over us; the eye of Allah is gazing upon us; by the power of Allah none shall overcome us;
And Allah encompasses them from behind: Nay, it is a noble recitation, in a guarded tablet.
For Allah is best as protector,
and He is the Most Merciful of the merciful.

These words are a prayer for refuge and Allah's support in the form of concealment and protection. *The veil of the Throne* is the perfect veil that covers all creation, for it is the ceiling of Paradise and the roof under which all the worlds are gathered.

The eye of Allah is His mercy and grace, which are directed to that which He looks upon. ʿAbd al-Malik ibn Marwān sent a threatening letter to al-Ḥajjāj, who in turn wrote to Ibn al-Ḥanīfiyya about it. His reply was: 'Allah looks upon His servants three hundred and sixty times every day; perhaps a single glance of these will fall upon me and be enough to save me from you.' Al-Ḥajjāj wrote this and sent it to ʿAbd al-Malik, who said: 'Such a reply can only have come from the prophetic Household!' Or he said something along those lines.

The Shaykh's words *By the power of Allah none shall overcome us* mean: By Allah's might, His servants will not be controlled or turned aside from His will. That is, none in existence shall overcome us either by natural or supernatural means.

﴾*Nay, it is a noble recitation*﴿ [85:21]; that is, a great and glorious one, ﴾*in a guarded tablet*﴿ [85:22]; that is, guarded from demons and other; or he may mean guarded against any tampering or alteration; and just as it is guarded, it guards.

He then recites the verse of protection: ﴾*For Allah is best as protector, and He is the Most Merciful of the merciful*﴿ [12:64]. That is, His protection is better than the protection afforded by material means and so on, for He is the Most Merciful of the merciful, and indeed there is no mercy but His mercy, and mercy is the source of protection; perfect protection comes from perfect mercy. Merciful people are those to whom the means of mercy are given, which in itself is a mercy from Him. ﴾*There is no god but He, the Compassionate, the Merciful*﴿ [2:163]. When mercy is ascribed to human beings, it is limited by their imperfections; were it not that mercy is ascribed to them in the Book of Allah and the words of His prophets, it would not be right to ascribe it to them at all. Indeed, the Prophet ﷺ said: '*Merciful people will be shown mercy by the Most Merciful on the Day of Resurrection. Show mercy to those on earth, and He in Heaven will show mercy to you.*'[86]

The verse tells us to leave aside material means and rely upon Allah when things are beyond our power to resolve; and this is the fundamental attitude to have. [Ibn 'Aṭā' Allāh] says in *al-Tanwīr*:

> The final word on this is that it is necessary for material means to exist, and also for there to be a way to see through them. Affirm them, inasmuch as He affirmed them in His

86 Narrated by al-Tirmidhī (*Jāmiʿ*, *al-Birr wal-Ṣila*, 1847) and Abū Dāwūd (*Sunan*, *al-Adab*, 4290).

wisdom; but do not rely on them, inasmuch as you know that He is One.

Understand this, may Allah have mercy on you, for it is the embodiment and epitome of the whole matter; and all success is from Allah.

﴾*Verily, Allah is my Patron, He who revealed down the Book;*
and He looks after the righteous.﴿
﴾*Allah is my Sufficiency, there is no god but He; on Him I rely,*
and He is Lord of the Mighty Throne.﴿
In the name of Allah, against whose Name
nothing can cause harm in the earth nor the sky;
and He is the All-Hearing, the All-Knowing.
There is no power, and no strength,
save by Allah, the High, the Great.

Since, in the passage preceding this, the Shaykh spoke of his reliance on Allah, and how all besides Allah is worthless, he expresses in this passage his detachment from everything but Allah, by his recourse to His patronage; for it is He who *looks after the righteous*, that is, those who detach themselves from everything but Him, and who seek the patronage of none but Him. He does not leave them to anyone else, for they have no desire for anyone but Him.

Shaykh Abū al-ʿAbbās al-Mursī ﷺ said: 'The saint's relationship to Allah is like that of the baby with his mother: does she leave him alone for someone to snatch?' Allah says: ﴾*As for those who take Allah as their patron, and His Messenger, and the believers: it is the party of Allah who shall surely triumph*❯ [5:56]. He also says: ❮*Whoso trusts in Allah, He is his sufficiency*❯ [65:3], that is, his provider, redeemer and helper.

The righteous are they whose states and deeds are right, such that their hearts are not right for anyone but Him, nor their bodies for anything but following His command. They are of different ranks, and they include His elite and His folk, namely they who have realised the true meaning of His words ❮*Allah is my Sufficiency*❯; that is, I am satisfied with Him, and ask for nothing else but Him, and ask for nothing from anyone but Him, because ❮*there is no god but He*❯, and no one else who deserves to be described by perfection but He. ❮*On Him I rely*❯ in all that I desire, ❮*and He is Lord of the Mighty Throne*❯ [9:129], so I love no one but Him. As Joseph, the Honest One ﷺ, said: 'I shall not leave the prison; for all that I need from your world is my religion, and all that I need from my religion is my Lord.'

He mentions the *Throne* and calls it *Mighty* because the one who possesses something mighty must necessarily be mightier than it.

His words *There is no power, and no strength, save by Allah, the High, the Great* mean that there is no movement nor stillness save by Allah: by His leave, and by His power. A hadith says: '*There is no power to avoid disobeying Allah save by Allah's protection, and no strength to obey Allah save by Allah's aid.*'[87] Another hadith says: '*It is one of the treasures of Paradise, and it wards off seventy kinds of tribulation, the least of them being worry.*'[88]

It is said that 'one of the treasures of Paradise' means that it is

87 Narrated by al-Najjār on the authority of Ibn Masʿūd ؓ (*Kashf al-Khafāʾ*, 840).

88 Narrated in a similar version by al-Tirmidhī (*Jāmiʿ, al-Daʿawāt*, 3525) and al-Suyūṭī (*al-Jāmiʿ al-Ṣaghīr*, 1828).

the source of contentment and resignation, which constitute the Paradise of this life. 'Abd al-Wāḥid ibn Zayd (may Allah have mercy on him) said: 'Contentment is Allah's greatest door, and the means by which His servants attain peace; it is the Garden of Bliss.' Allah Himself says: ❮*Whosoever does a righteous deed, be they male or female, and is a believer, We shall assuredly give them to live a goodly life*❯ [16:67]. It is said that this means a life of contentment in Allah, or a life of satisfaction.

The reason Allah described His Friends by saying that ❮*no fear shall be on them, nor shall they grieve*❯ [10:62] is that they have surrendered themselves unto Allah, and are content with Him; they choose only what He chooses. And when one is in such a state, there is no room for fear or grief; and Allah knows best.

We have already seen the meaning of *the High, the Great* at the beginning of the book, so look to it there [p. 44].

The Shaykh repeats these invocations three times because, as we said earlier, the Sunna of personal prayer and invocations of refuge and protection, and the like, is to repeat them three times; and Allah knows best.

A hadith says: '*Whoso says* ❮*If they turn away, say: Allah is my Sufficiency, there is no god but He; on Him I rely, and He is Lord of the Mighty Throne*❯ [*9:129*] *seven times after the dawn prayer, will have his sufficiency from Allah for that day, even if he is not truthful in the reliance he proclaims; and if he says it in the evening, he will have the same until morning.*'[89] 'Abd al-Malik ibn Ḥabīb related that if one recites it ten times in the morning, Allah will give him sufficient protection against all the evil of His creation, and the same for the evening. The first version is authentic, or close to it,

89 A similar version is narrated by Abū Dāwūd (*Sunan, al-Adab*, 4418).

unlike the second.

And all success is from Allah.

CONCLUSION – PART ONE

Concerning the issue of belief, criticism and imitation

Know that belief [*iʿtiqād*] is the root of all goodness, and criticism [*intiqād*] is the root of all evil. That said, the condition of valid belief is that one not be deluded, and the condition of valid criticism is that one do no harm. Shaykh Abū Madyan ﷺ said, according to what I have heard from some of the masters, 'Believe, and do not criticise, and do not put your trust in just anyone.' The jurist Abū ʿAbdallāh al-Maghribī (may Allah have mercy on him) said, 'Belief is sainthood, and criticism is a crime. If you understand, then follow; if you do not understand, then pass over in silent acceptance.'

The basis of Sufism is submission and trust, just as the basis of jurisprudence is investigation and research. For us, the principle is to think the best until there is just cause to do otherwise, while for the jurists it is the opposite, until there is cause to do otherwise. Yet it is necessary for all to be cautious until one is sure that no harm need be feared. Thus if you believe in someone, you should not follow him until you are sure of his knowledge and his religiosity; after that, it will not harm you if you see any flaw of his emerge, as long as you neither imitate him in it or abandon him because of it; and all success is from Allah.

In this time, there are many who call themselves shaykhs without having the right to, and many who attach themselves to worthless figures. Some people with attachments to spiritual chains have made a mockery of their religion, while others who claim spiritual authority have nullified their own faith. Some people have made it their business to deny absolutely everyone, and have thereby harmed themselves; others have preferred to pass over in silent acceptance, and have therefore been kept safe from all that they have brought. Some people have followed the way of extreme zealousness to their predecessors, and some of these have been destroyed and ruined by their zeal. Pass over things in silence and you shall be safe; cleave to Allah, hold fast to the Sunna and stand with the truth, and you will be allowed to drink from the waterholes of the true Men; and all success is from Allah.

Know, furthermore, that to imitate people is to become one of them, while to fail to do as they do is to become distant from them. To love the Sufis without following them does not bring any benefit.

In sum, he who aims to follow one of Allah's saints [*awliyā'*] must imitate his way in its fundamentals and important branches, but not necessarily in its minute details. He must also believe that this saint is a door to Allah, and stand by him so that through this door can blow to him the breezes of divine Mercy according to his intention; and his aim should be Allah alone and nothing else. He should venerate the saint and be of the view that Allah is pleased with him, because He replaces His saint when he is absent, and enriches through him when he is present. Mentioning the saint gives light to the heart, and seeing him opens doors to the unseen. We have spoken about this at length in other books as well as this one, so look to it there; and Allah guides to what is true and right.

CONCLUSION – PART TWO

The valid areas of imitation, what it brings, and its ruling

Know that imitation can be in dress, character and conduct. Imitation in dress is permitted in order to ward off harm and the like, for Allah says, ﴿*Tell your wives and daughters, and the believing women, to draw their garments over themselves; that makes it likelier that they will be recognised and not abused...*﴾ [33:59]. Thus He permitted wearing certain clothes to ward off harm. Donning the patched garment [*khirqa*] of the Sufis to join them by way of imitation is an example of this, but only on condition that one avoid sins both major and minor as well as all those things that are enjoyed by people of low moral character.

Now the one who imitates or follows a saint is either a lover [*muḥibb*] or a seeker [*ṭālib*]. The reward of the lover is that he becomes respected: reverence for him is placed in people's hearts so that anyone who sees him respects and venerates him. The reward of the seeker is that he is given counsel and help so that it becomes easy for him to do good deeds and forsake evil ones. All this is commensurate with his effort, will and aspiration; the more resolute people are, the more they can achieve.

The requirement of the shaykh who is followed is that he gives counsel to all as far as he is able, guiding them to God-consciousness and righteousness, and warding them away from evil and sin. He should pray for those of them who are accepted and ask Allah to keep them firm, and instruct them in their religion as best he can, and have compassion for them in their worldly affairs. For those of them who successfully abstain from falsehood, he should pray that they be given continued success. He should put as much effort into this as he does with his own self, because the host owes hospitality to his guest. He should also look to all of Allah's creatures with the eye of mercy, as is said:

My son, have mercy on all creatures,
And look upon them with kindness and compassion.
Venerate the elderly and have mercy on the young,
And fulfil the right of the Creator in those He created.

Imitation of character is one of the essentials of the spiritual path, and in conduct as long as this does not include special dispensations. If it is done with the special dispensations of the path such as spiritual audition [*samāʿ*] with all its proper conditions and is done by command, then the most that could be said about it is that it is disliked [*makrūh*]. If it goes outside its proper conditions, then it could stray into the unlawful because it constitutes misusing the truth and following that of which one has no knowledge. The author of *al-Mabāḥith al-Aṣliyya*, Ibn Banna of Saragossa, wrote a section on this subject that is required by every faithful believer; reading it and acting upon it is incumbent on every disciple – indeed, upon every believer who fears Allah and hopes for Him; and all success is from Allah.

CONCLUSION, PART THREE

How conduct should be imitated

The foundation of all this is to safeguard one's God-consciousness, which is done by fulfilling those things known to be obligatory and leaving those things known to be forbidden. It is then to be righteous, which means to adorn oneself with the perfections of character and realise the truth in all situations by renouncing vices, avoiding sins and rushing to do praiseworthy acts. This can only be achieved by doing three things: maintaining regular acts of worship [*iqāmat al-awrād*], seeking after the goal [*ittibāʿ al-murād*], and always preferring what is best [*īthār al-sadād*].

Maintaining regular acts of worship means to fill certain times with worship. The morning is for veneration, the late afternoon for dedication, and the night for communication. The final hours before dawn are the time for intimate discourse, invocation after the dawn prayer is the key to acts of obedience, and the time after the afternoon prayer is best for asking forgiveness from sin.

The balance of regular canonical prayer is a total of fifty cycles, both obligatory and sunna. The sunna prayers are six at midmorning [*ḍuḥā*], four before the midday prayer [*ẓuhr*] and two after, four before the afternoon prayer [*aṣr*], two after the sunset prayer [*maghrib*], and thirteen at night, starting with two short ones and ending with the *shafʿ* and *witr* prayers, which the Prophet ﷺ never left whether he was at home or abroad. Sometimes he might do less or more [at night]; say as few as seven or as many as seventeen. Then there are two before the dawn prayer [*ṣubḥ*]. The obligatory prayers contain seventeen cycles, from the midday prayer to the dawn prayer.

There are authentic narrations encouraging invocation after the obligatory prayers in general, and after the dawn prayer until the sun rises, and before sunset. The teaching of the Sunna about this are well known, and the forms it can take are numerous. Let us now conclude by mentioning some of them. We seek aid from Allah, and He is our Sufficiency and the best of guardians.

SOME CONCLUDING ADVICE

The first thing required of the one who is true to Allah is to follow the Sunna, and acknowledge His blessings and avoid vice and heretical innovation.

When waking from sleep, say: 'Praise be to Allah who has given us life after causing us to die; and to Him will be the return. We have reached morning, and all sovereignty belongs to Allah. Praise be to Allah, Lord of the Worlds. O Allah, we ask You for the goodness of this day and its success, aid, light, blessing and guidance, and we seek refuge with You from the evil of this day, the evil of what it contains and the evil that lies ahead of it.'

When leaving the house, say, 'In the Name of Allah. I trust in Allah. There is no power and no strength save by Allah, the High, the Almighty' three times, for it is a sufficiency, a guide and a protection.

Say, 'In the Name of Allah' when entering the lavatory, for it provides a veil between the jinn and the private parts of man.

When making ablutions, say, 'O Allah, forgive me my sins, and give me comfort in my home, and bless me in my provisions' during it and then again at the end after saying, 'I testify that there is no god but Allah, One without partner, and I testify that Muḥammad ﷺ is His servant and messenger. O Allah, make me one of those who repent, and one of those who purify themselves.' Then finish by saying, 'Glory be to You, Allah, and praise be to You. I testify that there is no god but You. I ask Your forgiveness and repent to You.'

When entering the mosque, say, 'In the Name of Allah, and may peace be upon the Messenger of Allah. O Allah, forgive me my sins and open for me the doors to Your mercy.' Enter with the right foot first and leave with the left, the opposite of entering and leaving the lavatory. As for the house, one enters and leaves with the right foot first.

In the two sunnas before the dawn prayer, recite *Sūrat al-Kāfirūn* and *Sūrat al-Ikhlāṣ* after the *Fatiha*, and then say after the prayer, 'O Allah, I ask You by Your blessed Countenance for Your gift of wellbeing and the completion of Your favour', three times, and then: 'O Allah, make light for me in my heart, light for me in my grave, light for me in my hearing, light for me in my sight, light for me in my hair, light for me in my skin, light for me in my flesh, light for me in my bones, light in front of me, light behind me, light to my right, light to my left, light above me, light below me. O Allah, increase me with light, and give me light, and make for me light.'

Then after the dawn prayer, say: 'O Allah, You are Peace, and from You is peace. Blessed are You, O Lord of Majesty and Bounty' once, and then 'Glory be to Allah', 'Praise be to Allah' and 'Allah is Greatest' thirty-three times each, completing the hundred with 'There is no god but Allah, One without partner. Dominion is His, praise is His, and He has power over all things. No one can withhold what You give, and no one can give what You withhold, and no one can turn back Your decree. The fortune of the fortunate avails nothing against You', once. Then supplicate for as long as you wish, and recite the *Āyat al-Kursī*, *Sūrat al-Ikhlāṣ*, *Sūrat al-Falaq* and *Sūrat al-Nās*. Do this after every other obligatory prayer as well. Finish all this with ﴾*Glory be to your Lord, the Lord of Might, beyond what they attribute to Him, and peace be upon the messengers, and praise be to Allah, Lord of the Worlds*﴿ [37:180–182]. The dawn and sunset prayers also have the following addition: 'There is no god but Allah, One without partner. Dominion is His, and praise is His. He gives life and deals death, and He is the Lord of the Mighty Throne' ten times, and then, 'O Allah, bless Muḥammad and his Family' ten times. After the dawn prayer, one should then stay in one's place and invoke until the sun has risen completely or almost completely.

Other things that can be invoked at that time are:

- reciting *Sūrat al-Ikhlāṣ*, *al-Falaq* and *al-Nās* three times morning and evening gives protection from all things;
- saying 'I seek refuge with the perfect Words of Allah from the evil of what He created' three times morning and evening, which gives protection from the harm of poisonous snakes, and safety to the traveller: if he says it when he makes camp, nothing will harm him until he resumes his journey;
- saying 'In the Name of Allah, against whose Name nothing can cause harm in the earth nor the sky; and He is the All-Hearing, the All-Knowing' three times in the morning and evening protects one from sudden tribulations;
- saying 'I seek refuge with Allah, the All-Hearing and All-Knowing, from the accursed Satan' three times along with the last three verses of *Sūrat al-Ḥashr* in the morning gives protection until evening;
- saying 'Glory be to Allah the Almighty, and praise be

to Him' three times after the dawn prayer and after the sunset prayer gives protection from leprosy, madness and paralysis;

- saying 'Glory be to Allah and praise be to Him according to the number of His creations, the contentment of His Self, the weight of His Throne and the ink of His Words' three times has a great worth;
- saying 'Glory be to You, Allah, and praise be to You. I testify that there is no god but You. I ask Your forgiveness and repent to You' expiates the sins of a gathering and puts blessing in it;
- saying 'I ask forgiveness of Allah the Almighty, besides whom there is no god, the Living and All-Sustaining, and I repent to Him' three times morning and evening expiates the sins of the day and the night;
- saying 'O Allah, bless our master Muḥammad, Your servant and prophet and messenger, the Unlettered Prophet, and his Family and Companions, and give them peace' three times is an expression of one's love for the Messenger of Allah ﷺ and one's yearning for him, and this will merit his intercession.

All this is related in accepted hadiths, along with other invocations we have compiled in a single litany for our companions, wherein we provided its source texts in a separate treatise of ours.

In addition to this, if you have more time than you can say, 'There is no god but Allah, One without partner. Dominion is His, praise is His, and He has power over all things' one hundred times, because this leads to forgiveness, increase and an ascension to higher ranks. No one could do anything greater than it, and it is a protection from every evil. There is also, 'Glory be to Allah and praise be to Him' one hundred times, and 'Glory be to Allah the Almighty and praise be to Him' one hundred times. They are all correct and authentic. Then there are the Enduring Acts of Good [*al-bāqiyāt al-ṣāliḥāt*]: 'Glory be to Allah, praise be to Allah, there is no god but Allah, Allah is Greatest, there is no power and no strength save by Allah, the High, the Almighty.' If you invoke all this one hundred times, you can combine the first glorification with the second ['Glory be to Allah and praise be to Him, Glory be to Allah the Almighty']. So these are three phrases that actually contain eight separate invocations; when added to one hundred prayers for forgiveness and one hundred blessings on the Messenger of Allah ﷺ, this makes a total of one thousand invocations.

You should then supplicate for as long as you wish, and read whatever portion of the Qur'an you are able. You should devote all your time to Allah in whatever way you can. Do not neglect to seek knowledge and earn a lawful livelihood, and leave aside all that does not concern you; this is the foundation.

Before sleeping, recite *Sūrat al-Ikhlāṣ*, *al-Falaq* and *al-Nās* after saying, 'In Your Name, Allah, I lay down on my side, and through You I shall raise it. O Allah, if You take my soul, then forgive it; and if You send it back, then give it the same protection You give Your righteous servants.' Then say, 'I ask forgiveness of Allah the Almighty, besides whom there is no god, the Living and All-Sustaining, and I repent to Him' three times, for it has been authentically related that this expiates one's sins even if they are as numerous as the foam of the sea, the sands of the dunes, the leaves of the trees and the days of the world.

When you wake up from your night's sleep, say, 'There is no god but Allah, One without partner. Dominion is His, praise is His, and He has power over all things,' and 'Glory be to Allah, praise be to Allah, there is no god but Allah, Allah is Greatest, there is no power and no strength save by Allah, the High, the Almighty.' After saying this if you supplicate, you will be answered; if you ask forgiveness, you will be forgiven; if you pray, your prayer will be accepted. This has been authentically narrated from the Messenger of Allah ﷺ.

Know that the foundations of goodness are three in number:

- fearing Allah in public and private;
- being content with Allah in poverty and wealth;
- virtue of character in all matters.

The Prophet ﷺ said, *'Be conscious of Allah wherever you are, and follow up bad deeds with good ones to erase them, and treat people with a goodly character.'*[90] Shaykh Abū al-Ḥasan said, 'Make God-consciousness your homeland, and then you will not be harmed by the foolishness of your soul, as long as you do not become contented with flaws, persist in sins or lose your fear of Allah when you are alone.'

Know also that all tribulation is combined in three things:

- fear of created beings;
- worry about one's provision;
- self-satisfaction.

And all health and goodness are combined in three things:

- trust in Allah in all things;
- contentment with Allah at all times;
- avoiding the evils of people whenever possible.

The one who trusts in Allah will not feel the need to rely on anyone else in anything he does, nor will he look to anyone else

90 Narrated by al-Tirmidhī (*Sunan, al-Birr*, 1910).

expecting benefit or harm. The one who is content with Allah will not grieve for what he loses, nor rejoice in what comes to him, nor look to the future or the past. The one who avoids the evils of people keeps his own evil away from them, and thereby is safe from their evil.

Shaykh Abū al-Ḥasan said, 'My beloved counselled me, saying: "Do not take a single step except where you might hope for the reward of Allah, and do not sit except where you are as secure as you can be from the disobedience of Allah. Keep the company of only those who aid you in the obedience of Allah, and choose not for yourself except those who increase you in certainty – and how rare they are!"'

He also said, 'My master advised me: "Beware of people! Purify your tongue from mentioning them, and your heart from hoping for their favour. Guard your extremities and perform your obligations, and you will attain saintly friendship [*wilāya*] with Allah. Never mention them except when the right of Allah upon you demands it, and your piety will be complete." And he said, "O Allah, preserve me from mentioning them, and from the obstacles they present, and save me from the evil of them, and suffice me with Your goodness over theirs, and distinguish me from among them. Indeed, You have the power to do anything!"'

He also said, 'I despaired of ever being able to benefit myself on my own, so why shouldn' I despair of anyone else benefitting me? I hope for Allah for the sake of others, so why shouldn' I hope for Him for myself?'

He also said, to someone who asked him about alchemy, 'Do not hope that Allah will give you anything other than what He has apportioned for you, and do not hope that any man can benefit you or harm you.'

The only way to attain this is to imagine that no one exists apart from you and your Lord. Leave aside all mankind and what has been destined for them, and work always towards being sincere before Him. Junayd ؓ was asked, 'How is it possible to detach oneself and be devoted to Allah alone?' He said, 'With repentance that puts an end to persistence in sin, fear that puts an end to procrastination, hope that inspires one to action, and breaking down the soul by reminding it of imminent death and removing it from vain hopes.' Someone asked, 'How can the servant reach this?' He replied, 'With a concentrated heart filled with pure *tawḥīd*.'

He ؓ also said, 'When a man points to the Real but attaches himself to other people, He causes him to need them but removes mercy for him from their hearts.'

He ؓ was asked about beneficial knowledge, and replied, 'It is to know your Lord, and not to object to your fate.'

He ؓ also said, 'I do not think that all the worldly things that come to me are bad, for I have made a principle for myself: the world is all evil, and is well able to send me everything that I dislike. If it happens to send me everything that I love, then this is a gracious gift; otherwise, the principle remains what it is.' This principle allows one to be wary and cautious of people, and think the best of them at the same time; and Allah knows best.

Addendum

Some important matters that people following the spiritual path require, whether they be in the world of isolation or the world of means[91]

Know, may Allah grace you and us with success, that being wary of evil and tribulation, and familiarising oneself with the reality of a time and its people, is the most crucial of things and the key to all goodness and righteousness. Ḥudhayfa ﵁ said, 'The people used to ask the Messenger of Allah ﷺ about goodness in all its form, while I used to ask him about evil. I asked him, "Will there be any good after this evil?" He said, "*Yes, but it will be cloudy.*" I said, "What will be the nature of this cloudiness?" He said, "*People who are guided by other than my guidance; some things from them you will recognise, and others you will reject.*" I said, "O Messenger of Allah, describe them for us." He said, "*They will be of our race, and speak our language.*" I said, "What do you command me to do if I encounter them?" He said, "*Stick with the*

91 This is *tajrīd* (isolation) and *asbāb* (means of causality). The person in *tajrīd* withdraws from society and devotes himself solely to the spiritual life, while the one in *asbāb* lives in society, earns a living and carries on the spiritual life at the same time. This is not something that is chosen by the disciple, but something chosen for him by Providence.

main group of the Muslims and their imam." I said, "What if they have no main group and no imam?" He said, "*Then withdraw from all of those groups, even if you have to gnaw upon the root of a tree until death comes to you while you are doing so.*"' This was narrated by al-Bukhārī and others.

The meaning of 'main group' [*jamāʿa*] here is the way of the majority of the People of the Sunna and their pious scholars. This is the way of earnestness and the manifestation of the Sunna, whose reality is not doubted by anyone but the deceived and the despised. It is centred on three things:

- leaving sins through God-consciousness and repentance;
- adhering to righteousness by following and preserving;
- fleeing from faults of any kind.

I have reflected on the tribulations of this time that afflict many Sufi dervishes [*fuqarāʾ*] and jurists [*fuqahāʾ*], and found that they amount to ten things:

[1] The first is being quick to perform excessive acts of voluntary worship while neglecting to fulfil obligations. One of them might stay up all night praying, but fail to perform the obligatory prayer properly. He might be regular in performing the midmorning [*ḍuḥā*] prayer and so on, but nonchalantly delay the obligatory prayer until its time is almost over. He might give a lot of money away in charity, but not give zakat to its proper recipients. He might fast often, seeking its virtue, but then backbite other Muslims freely without even thinking about it. All of this is born of following caprice and falling short of sincerity. Ibn 'Aṭā' Allāh said in the *Ḥikam*, 'A sign of following caprice is being quick to perform excessive acts of voluntary worship while neglecting to fulfil obligations.' Muḥammad ibn al-Wardī ﷺ said, 'People come to ruin because of two things: engaging in voluntary worship

while neglecting the obligatory, and acting with the body without engaging the heart. Allah does not accept an action unless it is sincere and in conformity with the truth.' This is an allusion to Allah's words ﴾*and exhort one another unto truth, and exhort one another unto patience*﴿ [103:3]. Another example of this is to suffice oneself with repenting, without putting right what one has done wrong and giving people back what is rightfully theirs, as is done by many ignorant people; and all success is from Allah.

[2] Often, disciples in their early stages will seek out different kinds of virtuous actions and act on unusual narrations, seeking to stack up virtuous deeds of all varieties. This only invites troubles and tribulations, because seeking out varieties of virtuous deeds amazes the soul and breaks the concentration of the heart, leading to languor and laziness, and ultimately to heretical innovations and deviations from the truth. Leave aside unusual narrations and doubtful matters, and follow the way of seriousness, namely those things that have a firm basis and substance to them. Leave other people to what they are doing, for that is what the Real wills for them. Every person I have ever seen go searching after all varieties of virtuous deeds has ended up falling into many forbidden things such as rebelling against leaders or sowing dissent among the Muslims. Everyone who acts on unusual narrations ends up falling into all kinds of tribulation, and everyone who searches after all varieties of virtuous deeds ends up falling into heretical matters, such as acting on forged hadiths. Shaykh Abū ʿAbdallāh al-Bilālī ﷺ said, 'It is forbidden to narrate a forged hadith unless it is in order to draw attention to its forgery, and it is forbidden to act on a forged hadith under any circumstance. This includes the pseudo-prayers some forged hadiths recommend for certain times or days of the week, or the narrations purportedly from Ubayy ibn

Kaʿb about the virtues of every chapter of the Qur'an, one after the other. Those exegetes who mentioned this in their works were mistaken.'

[3] Most disciples in this time, save for those whom Allah has protected, fall into three things:

- being deluded by everyone who makes a claim;
- following misgivings;
- taking pride in the *ṭarīqa*.

As for being deluded by claimants, it results from ignorance about this time and the people who live in it, and it leads to misguidance. As for following misgivings, Shaykh Abū ʿAbdallāh al-Bilālī said, 'A misgiving [*waswasa*] is essentially an innovation rooted in ignorance of the Sunna and misunderstandings of doctrine. It can be dispelled by ignoring it and continuously saying, "Glory be to Allah, the King, the Creator", ﴾*If He willed, He could do away with you all and bring forth a new creation; and such would not be difficult for Allah*﴿ [35:16–17].' As for taking pride in the *ṭarīqa*, it is born of foolishness and ignorance of what the *ṭarīqa* actually is. The spiritual path is built on humility and lowliness, until Allah brings them glory from Himself, and on poverty until He brings them wealth, without any self-regard or pride. The true dervish [*faqīr*, literally 'pauper'] is someone whose possessions are always ripe for the taking, and whose blood is cheap, and who suffices himself with Allah and looks to no one but Him. Indeed, he delights in humility and poverty. This was how the early Muslims were (may Allah be pleased with them). The true Sufis look upon all of Allah's creatures with mercy; they do not criticise them or blame them, never mind being rancorous towards them or looking down on them with pride. This is why Sahl ibn ʿAbdallāh ﷺ said, 'This path of ours befits only those whose souls are like brooms sweeping up refuse from the floor.' Al-Shiblī ؓ said, 'Since they deem the soul to be a natural pagan, they do not fight for it, since a believer should not be killed on account of an unbeliever.' Many other sayings could be quoted on this subject, but we would digress too much by doing so, so look them up; and all success is from Allah.

[4] Many dervishes of this time have become obsessed with gaining knowledge of secrets, experiential mysteries and the subtle profundities of the Sufis, without taking care to live up to the requirements of proper worship and good etiquette with Allah. Thus they have strayed away from the true goal and disconnected themselves from the path to Allah's love. The result of this is that they are hindered while displaying the guise of righteousness. Some of them are delighted when they understand something that the Sufis say, and mistake this for actual experience of it, even going as far as to claim that they have realised this spiritual state, when in fact they have been barred from it. The sincere man ought to busy himself with perfecting his character, attachment and realisation, and ignore all distractions. Ibn 'Aṭā' Allāh says in the *Ḥikam*, 'To be curious about the flaws hidden within you is better than being curious about the mysteries hidden outside you.' The Sufis have said, 'If the disciple speaks about a station he has not yet reached, he will be barred from reaching it, since he will have become one of those people who merely know about it. After that, he will not be safe from being misguided by it or getting lost in one of its symbols – that is what happens when one tries to take these things from the words of other people.'

One of the prime examples of this is obsession with mysterious sciences such as the sciences of Arabic letters and names, and the like. Knowledge of these sciences is attained by a divine gift and opening, and its experts only speak about it at all by way of aiding those who have been given such an opening and benefitting those who have already been shown the reality of them. Moreover, we have never seen or heard of anyone who truly gained or gave benefit through them on their own. May Allah have mercy on Shaykh Abū al-ʿAbbās al-Bannā who said,

> Be distinct from al-Būnī[92] and his like,
> And follow the example of Khayr al-Nassāj[93] and his like.

Likewise, Shaykh Muḥyī al-Dīn [ibn ʿArabī] said, 'The science of Arabic letters is a noble science learned by divine gift alone; actively seeking it is blameworthy for one's religion and worldly life.'

In sum, the sciences of divine gift are all praiseworthy in themselves, but blameworthy to seek. Only the ignorant seek them, and only the ignorant condemn them. Pass over them in silent acceptance, and you shall be safe. Avoid everything but invocation, and you will be saved from evil. By Allah, we have found all the secrets in invocation; we have not found them in the esoteric study of Arabic words, nor of non-Arabic words. Indeed, Mālik said to someone who asked him about it, 'How do you know it is not unbelief?'

It is true that the one who uses invocations needs to pay heed to their suitability in themselves as well their suitability vis-à-vis the times, strength of aspiration and strength of soul; but this is only known to the people of high aspiration and insight, and has

92 A contemporary of Ibn ʿArabī who wrote on the subject of the mystical properties of Arabic letters.

93 A member of the circle of Junayd.

mostly been lost in this time. Given that, you should stick to the Law and the outward elements of reality, and seek an opening from Allah through the strength of your spiritual aspiration; and all success is from Allah.

[5] Many of those who aspire to be dervishes in these times, and even those who aspire to be jurists, have become obsessed with studying the science of political forecasting [*ʿilm al-ḥidthān*], seeking treasures, performing alchemy and keeping the company of rulers and worldly people. All this is born of love for the world and desire for its baubles, and the heart being empty of the means to true success. Studying the science of political forecasting amounts to an attempt to spy on Allah in what He wills for the movements of time. It is rare for someone who engages in it to escape ruin by incurring the scourge of kings and turning them against him; even if he does escape this, he will not escape a life of misery because his pursuit will never lead him to any kind of goodness or comfort. It is even worse for the one who seeks this knowledge by means of astrology, because he is also compromising his belief to a greater or lesser extent. You know well what happens to those who spy on the kings of the earth – so what do you suppose will happen to the one who spies on the King of Kings? This is why you can barely find anyone engaged in this pursuit who does not suffer the tribulations of poverty, humiliation, misery and a bad death. The same is true for those who go searching for secrets, treasures and alchemy, because they are seeking to supplant Allah's wisdom in His creation with their own goals.

Likewise, keeping the company of worldly people and preferring them to the dervishes leads to immediate humiliation and eventual punishment. Avoid all of this and you will find safety for your religion and increase in your certitude; and all success is from Allah.

[6] Giving preference to spiritual audition [*samāʿ*], and gathering when there is no need or benefit, are useless, wasteful and born of weak certitude. Ibn al-ʿArīf said, 'They would not gather unless they had an issue to address, or worship to offer.' Shaykh Abū al-Ḥasan said, 'I asked my master about *samāʿ* and he answered me with Allah's words ﴾*They found their forefather erring, and rushed to follow in their footsteps*﴿ [37:69–70].' Shaykh Muḥyī al-Dīn said, 'The people of *samāʿ* and ecstasy [*wajd*] in this time have taken their religion as a game and a pastime, and so it is not permitted for any Muslim to promote *samāʿ* in this time, and no shaykh should be followed who does it or promotes it.' Shaykh Abū al-ʿAbbās al-Mursī said about Allah's words ﴾*They listen attentively to lies and devour what is forbidden*﴿ [5:42], 'The dervishes of this time who give preference to *samāʿ* and consume the wealth of tyrants have something in common with the Jews described in this verse, because they listen to songs of love but are not lovers, and listen to songs of ecstatic passion but do not experience it.' I am not sure of the exact wording of this, and he said more besides it; look for the passage in *Laṭāʾif al-Minan*.

[7] Many people busy themselves with curiosity and consider that they are doing something good. You find them saying, 'So-and-so is a perfected guide, and so-and-so is imperfect, and so-and-so has such-and-such spiritual station, and so-and-so has attained such-and-such, and so-and-so is a Pole [*quṭb*], and so-and-so is a Helper [*ghawth*], and so-and-so is one of the Substitutes [*abdāl*].' All of this is born of lack of shame, lack of manners and meddling in what does not concern one. The person who does it may rightly be called a liar, a false witness, a pretender and an aggressor, especially if he compounds this by calling truthful people liars or claiming things for himself that he does not have. Such a person

can truly be described by Allah's words ﴾*Who does more wrong than the one who utters a lie about Allah and rejects the truth when it comes to him?*﴿ [39:32]. Even worse than this is to compound it with self-regard by busying oneself with the faults of others and backbiting them, and meddling in other people's business by seeking news about rulers, the latest rumours, and stories about people's doings. The one who does this gathers up every evil, harm and blemish. This is the state of many people who have little piety, yet see themselves as being among the people of special status! May Allah give us refuge and protection from this, by His blessing and generosity.

[8] There are those who hope to attain spiritual perfection yet are lax with their religious affairs. One of them might aspire to high stations and seek to have the Supreme Name of Allah opened to him and benefit from seeing and keeping the company of the masters – yet he does not renounce unlawful things, or perform his prayers or preserve any of his religious affairs. This is like a man who cooks a block of frozen water and hopes to find meat in the pot. Allah has made the shaykh a guide, not a creator; He has given him the power to help, not to bring things into existence out of nothing. A man came to Shaykh Abū Muḥammad ʿAbd al-Salām ibn Mashīsh ﵁ and said, 'Master, instruct me with some regular litanies and actions.' The master became angry with him and said, 'Am I a divine messenger? As for the obligations, honour them; as for the prohibited things, refuse them. Protect your heart from desire for this world and love for women.' Look it up, as I am not sure of the exact wording. It is given in the book *al-Qaṣd ilā Allāh* attributed to Shaykh Abū al-Ḥasan, although he did not actually author it.

Another man said to him, 'Master, I ask you for permission to struggle against my soul.' He ﷺ replied by quoting, ﴾*They who believe in Allah and the Last Day do not ask you to excuse them from struggling with their possessions and their lives; and Allah knows who is conscious of Him. Only those ask you to excuse them who believe not in Allah and the Last Day, and whose hearts are in doubt, so that they waver in their doubt, back and forth*﴿ [9:44–45].

All of this comes from seeking dispensations and interpretations, and from ignorance and innovation in religion. This is why some people make it too hard for themselves, and others make it too easy; both of them are contravening the straight path. Only those whom Allah protects are spared from this, and they are rare indeed. It is related in the *Ṣaḥīḥ*: *'You will follow the ways of those who came before you, hand-span by hand-span and cubit by cubit. Even if they were to go into a lizard's hole, you would follow them into it.'* They said, 'O Messenger of Allah, do you mean the Jews and Christians?' He said, *'Who else?'*[94] Qāḍī Abū Bakr ibn al-ʿArabī said, 'By the lizard-hole, he was alluding to the fact that they will be followed in their narrowness and strictness.' This is clear; and all success is from Allah.

[9] Some people fall into inventing new modes of action and the like, and following those who invent them. This must be renounced completely in favour of that which is clearly rightly-guided and based on the way of precaution, and nothing besides. This can only be done by realising knowledge and practice of the texts of the Sacred Law and the deductions of the imams. The imams and scholars of Islam have warned against this, such as Qāḍī Abū Bakr ibn al-ʿArabī (may Allah have mercy on him) in the chapter on the middle night of Shaʿbān in his book *al-Āriḍa*,

94 Narrated by al-Bukhārī (*Ṣaḥīḥ, al-Anbiyā'*, 3199).

where he said: 'Know, may Allah have mercy on you, that I wish to tell you that because of people's ignorance of the truth and desire for goodness, Allah has unleashed upon them people who are respected as people of knowledge though they do not deserve this, and they have attributed hadiths to the Prophet ﷺ for which Allah sent down no authority, and they have presented evil things to them in the guise of good things in order to make them people whose deeds lead to nothing but loss. They are servants of Satan, not servants of the Compassionate ... The worshipper should be cautious not to take anything that is not in the five books of Islam: *Bukhārī*, *Muslim*, *Tirmidhī*, *Abū Dāwūd* and *Nasāʾī*.' He also said that the *Muwaṭṭā* is the spirit and crown of all of them; look it up if you wish to read further.

[10] Many people believe that the shaykhs have been granted infallibility [*ʿiṣma*] and rely on them completely as intermediaries between them and their Lord, deeming that they must be followed in all things whether they are lawful or not. Others, on the contrary, criticise shaykhs for doing things that are not even unlawful, or discount them entirely for making one or two mistakes. Some consider a person's knowledge or title of shaykh to be enough to affirm realisation, or consider a miraculous gift [*karāma*] as reason enough to follow him, or indeed any supernatural event at all, or even consider any unusual thing whatsoever to be enough. Some only believe in those who are divinely attracted [*majdhūb*] or insane, and others are the opposite. Some people will say whenever anyone is mentioned to them, 'May Allah benefit us through the righteous.' Some people only take the dead as their shaykhs and disregard the living, while others do the opposite. Some people only rely on stories they hear from elders, and if they do not find such stories about someone, they belittle him. Some

people use themselves as the benchmark: if someone is generous, respectful and kind to them, they deem them to be saints and spiritual guides; and if they do not witness any miracles from a person, nor does he treat them with special kindness or generosity, they do not accept him or approach him. Indeed, most people just want someone who will change nature for them, or reveal the unseen to them, or go against wisdom, or violate the sanctity of the Law, or make vile displays.

In sum, caprice has taken over souls and the truth has been made the slave of caprice. Yet caprice is nothing but a shot in the dark. The intelligent person takes care to be aware of his time and the people who live in it, minds his own business instead of being curious. The Messenger of Allah ﷺ said to Abū Thaʿlaba al-Khushanī, *'When you see greed being obeyed, caprice being followed and everyone being pleased with his own opinion, then withdraw and concern yourself with your own soul.'*[95] When Abū Dharr ؓ asked him about what was in the scriptures of Abraham ؑ, he said, *'The scriptures of Abraham say: The intelligent man must know his time, hold his tongue and mind his own business. The intelligent man must reserve four times: a time for intimate discourse with his Lord, a time for reckoning his own soul, a time for allowing his soul to indulge in its lawful passions, and a time for being with his brethren who help him to see his own faults and guide him to his Lord.'*

Shaykh Abū al-Ḥasan ؓ said, 'My master (may Allah have mercy on him) counselled me, saying: "Do not keep the company of him who prefers himself to you, for he is wretched, nor of him who prefers you to himself, for he is rarely constant. Keep the company of him who, when he remembers, remembers Allah; for Allah will

---

95 Narrated by Ibn Mājah (*Sunan, al-Fitan*, 4004).

enrich through him when he is present, and replace him when he is absent. Mentioning him gives light to the heart, and seeing him opens doors to the unseen."'

He also said, 'I asked my master ﷺ about the Prophet's ﷺ words "*Make things easy and do not make them difficult; give people glad tidings and do not put them off.*" He said, "This means: Guide them to Allah and do not guide them to anything but Him; for the one who guides you to the world only cheats you, and the one who guides you to work only tires you out, while the one who guides you to Allah counsels you well."'

Guiding to Allah means three things:

- turning away from created beings in all things;
- turning to Allah in all things;
- raising one's aspiration above created beings in all things.

Shaykh Abū al-ʿAbbās al-Mursī ﷺ said, 'By Allah, I see no honour in anything except raising one's aspiration above created things.' He ﷺ also said, 'Security in religion is found by raising one's aspiration above created things.' Bishr ﷺ said, 'I saw ʿAlī ibn Abī Ṭālib ﷺ in a dream. I said, "O Commander of the Faithful, how good it is for the rich to treat the poor with compassion, hoping for reward from Allah!" He said, "Better still is for the poor to keep their dignity by turning down the offers of the rich, trusting in Allah."'Abū al-Qāsim al-Qushayrī ﷺ said, 'Greater than this is the aspiration of the gnostics, in which disappears not only all that is created, but all that is destined.'

Shaykh Abū al-Ḥasan ﷺ said, 'There are four matters of conduct; if the dervish who isolates himself for worship [*al-faqīr al-mutajarrid*] does not have it, then he is no better than dirt: mercy to the young, respect for the old, honesty with oneself and refraining from defending oneself. There are another four matters of conduct; if the initiated dervish [*al-faqīr al-muntasib*] does not have them, then pay no heed to him even if he be the most knowledgeable man on earth: keeping away from tyrants, preferring the people of the hereafter, comforting the poor and praying the five daily prayers in regular congregation.'

The Messenger of Allah ﷺ said to someone who asked him for counsel, *'Say, "Allah is my Sufficiency", and then be upright.'*[96] He said to another, *'Let your tongue remain moist with the remembrance of Allah.'*[97] To another he said, *'Do not become angry.'*[98] A man said, 'O Messenger of Allah, direct me to an action I can perform so that Allah will love me and the people will love me.' He said, *'Detach yourself from this world and Allah will love you; detach yourself from what people own and they will love you.'*[99] They say that detachment [*zuhd*] from this world is for the heart to grow dispassionate for it in all circumstances. A hadith says, *'Detachment is not attained by making the lawful unlawful or by squandering possessions; detachment is to be more confident in what is in Allah's hand than what is in your own.'*

Shaykh Abū al-Ḥasan ؓ said, 'I saw [Abū Bakr] al-Ṣiddīq in a dream. He said, "Do you know the sign that love of the world has left the heart? It is that one gives worldly things away freely when one has them, and feels relieved of them when one does not have them."' He ؓ also said, 'That Allah enrich you without the world is better than that He enrich you with it. By Allah, no one is ever truly enriched by it. How could they be, when Allah has said, ﴾*Say: 'The comfort of this world is paltry'*﴿ [4:77]?'

96 Narrated by al-Tirmidhī (*Sunan, al-Zuhd*, 2334) with *'Say: "Allah is my Lord..."'*
97 Narrated by al-Tirmidhī (*Sunan, al-Daʿawāt*, 3297).
98 Narrated by al-Bukhārī (*Ṣaḥīḥ, al-Adab*, 5651).
99 Narrated by Ibn Mājah (*Sunan, al-Zuhd*, 4092).

Know that all people work to enrich themselves with things, while the Sufis work to enrich themselves *without* things. This is why they come to be independent of things even as they seem to be in need of them; they seek things by despairing of them, and possess things by abstaining from them. The Prophet ﷺ said, *'Richness is not having many things; true richness is richness of soul.'*[100] The Sufis have said about this:

Be submissive to Allah, do not be submissive to people;
Be content with honour, for honour is in resignation.
Be independent of every relative and kinsman,
For richness is in being independent of people.

The Prophet ﷺ said, *'Be in the world as a stranger or a wayfarer; count yourself as one of the dead.'*[101] It is known that the stranger does not base his actions on any notion of stability, or demand anyone's loyalty. The one who knows what a stranger he is in the world will be naturally averse to it. The one who knows that death and destruction is his ultimate fate will never grow accustomed to anything in the world. The one who knows how lonely he will be in the grave will seek after anything that can give him company in it; and only his righteous deeds can do that. The one who knows that he will stand before Allah will be too ashamed to let Him see him do anything He has forbidden, or fail to do anything He has commanded. The one who knows his time and the people who live in it will cease to be concerned with it. The one who knows mankind and what they are will leave them to their own devices; he will not argue with anyone or criticise them, nor condemn or

100 Narrated by al-Bukhārī (*Ṣaḥīḥ, al-Riqāq*, 5965).
101 Narrated by Aḥmad (*Musnad, al-Mukthirīn*, 4534).

refute them; he will restrain himself completely and be as good to them as he can, and beware of them as well as he can. The Prophet ﷺ would beware of people and be on his guard from them without ever denying anyone his cheerfulness and good character. May Allah have mercy on Ibn ʿAṭāʾ Allāh, who said in *al-Tanwīr*:

Never concern yourself with criticising others,
  Wasting your time when time is short;
How can you criticise them, when you believe
  That all things happen as they were destined to?
True, they have not fulfilled Allah's right –
  Do you think *you* have fulfilled it, as wretched as you are?
Recognise the rights you owe them, and then act:
  Fulfil them all and be patient as you do it.
If you do this, then you are who you are
  In the eye of Him who knows all things.

One of the best descriptions of the virtue and importance of this attitude was offered by whoever said:

If you wish to live with your religion secure,
  Your portion assured and your reputation intact,
Do not ever speak about the blemishes of a man;
  For you too have blemishes, and others too can speak!
Say to your eye when it falls on such a thing,
  'O eye, do not look, for others too have eyes!'
Treat others well and avoid those who are contentious;
  By all means make distinctions – but in the best way.

Another thing that was said about self-control and detachment from the possessions of others, and has been attributed to Ibrāhīm al-Khawwāṣ ﷺ, is:

I bore some discomfort patiently, fearing the rest of it;
I restrained my soul, and thus it was given honour.
I gave it doses of what it hated until it was trained;
Before, such a dose would have utterly disgusted it.
Many an honour can humiliate the soul;
Many a soul can be honoured by humiliation.
If I extend my hand to seek riches from anyone
But Him who said, 'Ask Me', it will be paralysed.
I shall strive to be patient, for there is honour in patience,
And be content with what I get in this world though it be a little.

Another of our masters ﷺ conveyed to us the following counsel, attributing it to one of gnostics:

Live in obscurity among men, and be content with it,
For it is safer for this world and for religion.
Mingling with people threatens the spiritual life,
And causes one to be buffeted here and there.

He also quoted in a book he wrote about the knowledge and wisdom of the Sufis:

Expose yourself to Allah's breezes and stand by His door,
For it may be that the door will soon open.
Beware, beware again of leadership,
For it is the worst disease to afflict religion.
Be humble and buckle down, stay patiently by the door,
Strive against your soul and perhaps you will succeed.
Love for wealth and prestige is a foul doubt,
And is even fouler for the people of knowledge;
Love for poverty and detachment is a beautiful virtue,

And is even more precious and splendid for them.
Were they to reject me, I would be a slave for their slave,
Like a dog barking in a refuse heap.
Never seek support from the people of tyranny,
For you will be raised up with them, and cast into Hell.

One of the best things that have been said about devoting oneself to Allah, fleeing from all other than Him and leaving aside everything but Him is what was said by Shaykh Abū al-ʿAbbās Aḥmad al-Rifāʿī رضي الله عنه:

If only You are sweet when life is bitter;
If only You are pleased when the people are enraged;
If only my relationship with You can prosper,
While my relationship with the rest of the world is barren.
When Your love is truly felt, it all becomes so easy,
And everything above the dust is dust.

A FINAL WORD

Know that everything we have said in this conclusion, and indeed everything we have said in this book, is meant as a reminder, an alert and an outward lesson. The proper way to follow the spiritual path and act on it is first to make proper repentance with its three conditions of validity:

1. regretting what one has done;
2. ceasing to do it;
3. resolving never to do it again.

And its four obligations:

1. returning things that were unjustly taken;
2. avoiding forbidden things;
3. fulfilling rights;
4. correcting one's intention.

And its six compliments:

1. attaining God-consciousness through scrupulousness;
2. realising uprightness through honesty;
3. improving one's conduct by avoiding people while having compassion for them;
4. buckling down to righteous action;
5. turning away from distractions and laziness;
6. leaving all that is other than Allah, whatever it may be.

This is helped by three things:

1. refraining from being curious about everything;
2. being aware of Allah in everything;
3. leaving the unlawful and the doubtful in everything.

Those who eat what is lawful obey Allah whether they like it or not; those who eat what is unlawful disobey Allah whether they like it or not. A man is upon the religion of his close friend. So eat what you wish, and your actions will accord with it; and befriend whom you wish, and you will follow his religion. The believer is amiable and well-liked, attentive and cautious. Two times out of three, he ignores things.[102]

Repentance is aided and strengthened by much remembrance of Allah and invocations of blessings on the Messenger of Allah ﷺ, until the soul becomes permanently habituated to this; whereupon one moves on to invoking 'Glory be to Allah, and praise be to Allah', until the soul becomes permanently habituated to this; whereupon one moves on to invoking 'Glory be to Allah the Almighty, and praise be to Him'; until the soul becomes permanently habituated to this, whereupon one can combine the three by invoking 'Glory be to Allah and praise be to Him, glory be to Allah the Almighty', until the soul becomes permanently habituated to this; whereupon one moves on to invoking 'I ask forgiveness of Allah', until the soul becomes permanently habituated to this; whereupon one moves on to invoking the Enduring Acts of Good [*al-bāqiyāt al-ṣāliḥāt*]: 'Glory be to Allah, praise be to Allah, there is no god but Allah, Allah is Greatest, there is no power and no strength save by Allah, the High, the

102 Shaykh Zarrūq explains this in his *Qawāʿid* as meaning 'he ignores statements and opinions, but not actions; the Prophet ﷺ encouraged us to flee from tribulations' (*Qāʿida* no. 191).

Almighty.' These things purify the heart, and through their meanings the way is opened to spiritual opening and perfection, and the signs of success appear in the shortest time.

Know also that invocation does not have any effect unless it is accompanied by three things: conditioning one's physical nature through hunger, silence and lack of sleep, and fleeing from created beings. Moderation is required in all this, and it should be done according to need: the one for whom being hungry is more important than being full should not eat more than what he needs, but a little less; the one for whom silence is more important than speech should not speak about anything that does not directly concern him; the one for whom lack of sleep is more important than sleep should only take the bare minimum of sleep he needs; and the one for whom fleeing from created beings is more important than keeping their company should withdraw from them whenever he can. The one who is pure in his intention will be purified; the one whose intention is mixed will get mixed results.

One of the things our master Shaykh Abū al-ʿAbbās al-Ḥaḍramī ﷺ wrote to us in his first counsel was: 'Keep to constant remembrance and invocation of blessings upon the Messenger of Allah ﷺ, for this is a ladder, an ascension and a journey to Allah when the seeker cannot find a shaykh to guide him. The Messenger of Allah ﷺ said, "*When someone asks for forgiveness often, Allah gives him a release from every worry and a way out of every constraint, and provides for him from where he least expects it.*"[103] He ﷺ also said, "*Invoking blessings upon me is a light in the heart, a light in the grave and a light on the Bridge.*" The way to

103 Narrated by Ibn Mājah (*Sunan, al-Adab*, 3809).

approach invocation is to gather your thoughts and concentrate your heart on what you are about to do, and then begin invoking until the soul responds to it and the invocation takes hold of the soul in its entirety, so that whenever something comes to distract it or take it out thereof, the invocation protects the soul from it without even having to confront it; and all success is from Allah.'

It is now time to end with some prayers and blessings on the Messenger of Allah ﷺ, which is the beginning, the end and the entirety of all the matters of this world and the world to come; and all success is from Allah.

O Allah! We ask You for constant faith. We ask You for pious hearts. We ask You for beneficial knowledge. We ask You for firm religion. We ask You for health from every blight. We ask You for complete health. We ask You for constant health. We ask You for gratitude for health. We ask You for independence from other people.

O Allah! We ask You for knowledge that is beneficial, action that is righteous and accepted, provision that is ample and lawful, and lives that are long and blessed. We ask You for health in life and in religion. By Your mercy, O Most Merciful of the merciful!

O Allah! Broaden for us Your protection in this life and the next, and spread upon us Your mercy in them. Complete Your favour over us, O Most Generous of the Generous!

O Allah! We ask You for stable life, righteous action, ample provision, perfect health and encompassing favour, for we are in no way independent of Your goodness. By Your mercy, O Most Merciful of the merciful!

I ask forgiveness of Allah for my presumption and poor manners in being so bold as to speak about the words of Allah's saints. Allah is the patron of all who rely on Him, and the Sufficiency of all who turn to Him. He is our Sufficiency and the best of guardians.

The author, the needy servant of Allah, Aḥmad ibn Aḥmad ibn Muḥammad ibn ʿĪsā al-Burnusī al-Fāsī, known as Zarrūq, may Allah rectify his state and forgive his sins, says:

Here ends this treatise according to what Allah has provided for it. I hope that it will be accepted tolerantly and judged discriminately. Allah helps the servant as long as the servant helps his brother. Peace.

Also from Visions of Reality Books

Muḥammad ﷺ the Perfect Man

In this book Sayyid Muḥammad ibn ʿAlawī al-Mālikī, may Allah be merciful to him, writes with great erudition and love about the perfection of the last of the Messengers, Muḥammad ﷺ, sourcing every point from careful exegesis of *āyāt* of Qur'ān, well known hadith and episodes from the *sīrah*. Following in the esteemed footsteps of Qāḍī ʿIyād, whose universally respected *ash-Shifā* has always been the benchmark against which other such works are measured, Sayyid Muḥammad has nevertheless added immeasurably to this noble tradition and produced a genuinely new work of great insight and *bārakah*, may Allah reward him well.

Available from visions-of-reality.com and Amazon

Translated and edited by Dr. Mostafā al-Badawi

A Journey of Loving Hearts to the Master of Divine Envoys

A Guide to Visiting the Messenger of God and his Blessed Mosque

This is the definitive guide to visiting the Messenger of God, may peace and blessings be upon him, with high adab and courtesy the book takes the visitor to the Radiant City of Madina, and the Blessed Mosque of the Messenger of God, and onwards through to presenting oneself in front of the Best of Creation ﷺ.

En route the authors dedicate chapters to The Merits of the Possessor of the Tremendous Character, the Shariah position of visiting him, Attributes of the City of the Messenger of God and his blessed Mosque, Recommendations for the Visitor of Madina the Radiant, Names of the Chosen One, The Good Manners in Standing in the Presence of the Chosen One, How to Visit the Beloved ﷺ.

This is a tremendous work which will be a valuable addition to the traditional Islamic literature in the English language.

Available from visions-of-reality.com and Amazon